Toy train reference series: 1

LIONEL'S POSTWAR F3'S

By Joe Algozzini

With the assistance of Manny Piazza,
Frank Piazza, and Bob Jacobson

Published by Greenberg Books, a division of Kalmbach Publishing Co., 21027 Crossroads Circle, Waukesha, Wisconsin 53187. Phone: (414) 796-8776.

Printed in the United States of America

Publisher's Cataloging-in-Publication Data
(Prepared by Quality Books, Inc.)

Algozzini, Joseph P.
Lionel's postwar F3's / Joe Algozzini.
— Waukesha, WI : Greenberg Pub., 1995.
p. cm. — Toy train reference series ; 1)
ISBN 0-89778-398-0

1. Railroads—Models. I. Title.

TF197.A54 1995 625.1'9
QBI95-20354

Contents

ACKNOWLEDGEMENTS

A BOOK of this nature could not possibly be undertaken and completed by only one individual. It took the combined efforts of many. The majority of my research was completed with the assistance of Manny Piazza, Frank Piazza, and Bob Jacobson. I'm forever grateful for their assistance. I must also acknowledge my good friend Joe Bak's contribution for the repair and maintenance chapter.

As always Ed Dougherty, Mel Nicholas, Sid Brown, and Dennis Hult allowed inspection of their collections and also loaned many items to be photographed for this book. (Yes, I'll return the F3s; sorry to have kept them for so long.)

Dan Mega did much of the legwork in respect to Lionel individual boxes and master cartons; also instrumental in the box effort were Rich Wargowsky, Clark Vegazo, and Lew Striebeck. (No, you can't have my 2242 master carton.)

Special thanks are in order to Richie Shanfeld, who always seems to help me out with my projects. Thanks also to Bob Corbin, Ed Holderle, Rich Mack, Gary Mack, and Nick Mazzocchi.

Other collectors contributing to the project included Drew Bauer, Don Fiore, Joe Grzyboski Jr., Terrell Klaassen, Steve Lukefahr, Ernie Reising, Preston Richards, Ed Rowe, Charles Siegel, Don Shaw, Greg Stout, Bob Ford, Lee Price, Bob Caplan, Carl Hurschik, Dennis Schoup, and Doug Waller.

Ed Kraemer deserves thanks for providing samples of his repainted shells, and I want to acknowledge Paul Ambrose's work on box nomenclature and 3-digit set numbers.

Thanks also goes to Lionel Trains Inc. and members of their staff for allowing us to visit the archives and for assisting us in photographing many of the pertinent pieces there. Special thanks to my good friend Lenny Dean, who always has time for my questions.

Helpers at Kalmbach Publishing Co. include Dick Christianson, editor; Kristi Ludwig, designer; Mary Algozin, copy editor; Julie LaFountain, editorial assistant; Darla Evans and Jim Forbes, photographers; and Roger Carp, editor of *Classic Toy Trains* Magazine.

– *Joe Algozzini*

INTRODUCTION

COLLECTORS AND OPERATORS have long awaited a definitive work on Postwar Lionel trains. Unfortunately, no single volume alone can provide enthusiasts with all of the toy train information that has been uncovered over the past 25 years (or more) of Postwar collecting. Multiple volumes would be required. It is our intention, over time, to provide toy train enthusiasts with that series of books.

The first volume in our projected series is devoted to the most popular of all of Lionel's Postwar production: the F3 locomotives produced between 1948 and 1966. Every aspect of these locomotives that we believe to be significant and to which we have access will be covered in a manner that we hope is entertaining as well as informative.

For collectors:

- Complete chronology of F3s, including frames, trucks, couplers, etc.
- Information on fakes and repaints
- Listings of original boxes (individual, set, and master cartons)
- And much more.

For operators:

- Introduction to the real F3 locomotives on which Lionel's were patterned
- Helpful repair tips, including common problems
- Maintenance and lubrication tips and diagrams
- And more.

Perhaps the most significant *new* information this book will provide is about boxes. Original boxes can add considerably to the buying/selling price of a collectible train. Unfortunately, over the years individuals have – both intentionally and unintentionally – placed cars and locomotives in the wrong boxes. Unsuspecting buyers who pay a premium for those boxed trains have been shortchanged. The information this book provides can be looked at as a type of insurance designed to protect the enthusiast's investment and to make his or her collection "correct."

One key thing to keep in mind as you read this book, particularly the section on chronology of modifications: *every* year should be considered a *transition* year, as the previous year's parts – or inventory of leftover merchandise – can flow directly into the following year's production. For instance, the top of the F3 knuckle was embossed starting in 1954, and this was carried into 1955 and beyond. However, the reverse can never be true; an item used in any future year's production cannot exist in any prior year's production. That embossed knuckle known to have been first used in 1954 cannot show up in a verified 1953 product.

Remember that Lionel, like any other manufacturer, was producing a product, not a collectible that required each production run to be distinct and uniform. Lionel was producing a toy, to be sold at a profit, and (for the most part) could care less how last year's leftover inventory was used, other than that it be used up! Only the production manager knew when the coupler bin was empty and embossed ones were first poured in – and as difficult as it might be for collectors to imagine, he didn't really care.

Another source of confusion over what's "right" and what isn't is the repairs and changes made by service stations, hobbyshops, and others. Many times a much earlier – or later – frame, truck, or detail item was substituted simply because it happened to be handy or available. To the novice, the item still looks original. No deception was intended; trains were simply being repaired. However, as these trains made their way into the hands of operators, collectors, and dealers, those repairs or changes were accepted as "original." New owners assumed their trains came from the factory equipped that way.

For example, one of the more common changes made was that of replacing a post-1952 "bar-end" truck with a "staple-end" truck last manufactured during the 1951 production year. Another source of confusion resulted when a repairman exchanged a battery-damaged F3 frame with a frame from a different year. The shell is in great shape, the frame looks good, but together they're wrong. The owner thinks he has a "rare variation," when in fact all he has is a swapped frame.

Though years of exhaustive research and observation have contributed to this book, additional information is likely to become available as time passes. The author and publisher are interested in hearing from those readers who believe they can add to the F3 story. That information will be evaluated and, as appropriate, included in future editions or in a separate volume.

We hope you enjoy – and learn from – this first volume of our series detailing the history of Postwar Lionel trains.

OVERVIEW: 1948–1966

"Swift – Powerful – Magnificent" (1949 Lionel catalog)

THE STREAMLINING ERA in North American railroading began during the 1930s. Trains with names like *Zephyr, Hiawatha,* and *Super Chief* captured the imagination of young and old alike. These bullet-shaped trains, glistening in their stainless-steel sheathing, were to that generation what moon rockets and the space shuttle are to ours. Speed, power, adventure, drama – streamliners were all of these things formed into shiny pieces of machinery that hurtled across the country at speeds in excess of 100 m.p.h.

Only a few years earlier, the railroad industry had realized that steam locomotion, after a century of service, was old technology that needed to be set aside to make way for an emerging source of power: diesel. Cleaner to operate, requiring less maintenance, and providing more power, diesel engines would push aside steam within a matter of only a couple decades.

Before long, streamlined diesels began to take the place of steam engines as quickly as budgets and wartime constraints allowed. Steam engines disappeared from main lines first, and eventually branch lines gave up their "Ol' Smokeys."

By the mid-1950s, when most Americans thought of railroads they thought of streamlined diesels. In fact, many of them thought of Santa Fe F3s, in no small part because of the influence of Lionel toy trains.

THE REAL F3s

Santa Fe no. 18, resplendent in its red and yellow warbonnet, was photographed in Los Angeles in November of 1948 by Donald Sims. Notable are the portholes, screened panels along the side, and yellow stripe over the nose.

By the end of World War II, the days of the steam engine were numbered. The great conflict in Europe and the Pacific had given steam a temporary reprieve, but diesel-electric technology developed before the war would soon derail the old steamers. Sleek new diesel electrics were quickly taking their place at the head end of streamlined passenger trains while diesel switchers were shoving strings of freight cars around railroad yards across America.

General Electric, Ingersoll-Rand, American Locomotive Works, Baldwin Locomotive Works, Fairbanks-Morse, and Electro-Motive Division of the General Motors Corporation were all involved in the race to replace steam. The most successful of them was EMD.

With diesels handling yard switching and passenger trains, over-the-road freight traffic was about all that was left for steam engines to handle. And that was the manufacturer's next target.

EMD's first over-the-road freight diesel locomotive was the FT (for "freight"); in fact, the FT was America's first mass-produced road freight diesel locomotive. Manufactured between 1939 and 1945, these engines looked very much like stubby E units, and they proved to be very popular. In just six years, American railroads replaced war-weary steam engines with 1096 of these locomotives (555 A units and 541 B units).

In 1945 the first F3 locomotive, the engine upon which Lionel based its enormously successful model, rolled out of EMD's shops in LaGrange, Illinois. To the casual observer, the F3 and FT looked pretty much alike. Upon closer inspection, however, there were a lot of differences, both internal and external. The F3's engine produced 1500 h.p., compared to the FT's 1350; the F3 was about 3 feet longer than the FT; the F3 had only two exhaust stacks while the FT had four; and, depending on how it was equipped and when it was purchased, the F3 sported different combinations of side panels, filters, grills, and roof fans. In the short time during which it was produced (July of 1945 through February of 1949), 1107 A units and 694 B units were manufactured for railroads all across the United States, from the New York Central in the East to the Santa Fe in the West (six more were made for Canadian railroads).

The F3s were followed by F7s and F9s (produced through 1957), all of which carried the same general shape of the F3. In the U.S. alone, 3856 F7s and F9s were sold; Canada and Mexico bought another 234. Because of their versatility, F3s, F7s, and F9s were available equipped for both passenger and freight service. No other locomotive of the period came close to challenging the domination of the railroad industry like the mighty F. And no other locomotive was as visible to the general public; all totaled, EMD manufactured and sold 5897 (F3s, 7s, and 9s). If you saw trains, you were sure to see F units. There were other diesels, but that distinctive "bulldog" nose was the look that stuck in your mind.

What better choice of locomotive to be the flagship of Postwar Lionel's line of toy trains?

"The Finest Model *Diesels* in the World!" (1953 Lionel catalog)

The subject of our story, the mighty F3, rolled out of General Motors Corporation's Electro-Motive Division in LaGrange, Illinois, just as World War II was ending. (The earlier versions, FTs and F2s, had been produced from 1939 through 1946.) The F unit quickly became the locomotive of choice on North America's railroads. Between 1939 and 1957, EMD produced an astounding 7097 F-series locomotives.

But EMD was a piker compared to Joshua Lionel Cowen's company. The September 5, 1949, issue of *Life* magazine reported that Lionel produced 125 F3 diesels every hour during the holiday rush period. Given the amount of time required for research, drafting, modelmaking, tooling, testing, and all the other steps involved in bringing a new toy train to market, executives and engineers at the Lionel Corporation most likely started on the F-unit project soon after the war. Producing an O gauge model of a diesel locomotive may have come up during the Sunday meetings top management held during the war in preparation for the day when the company could get back to making toy trains instead of naval instruments. In any case, the F3 must have been among Lionel's earliest projects as soon as its role in war production was ended.

The first Lionel F3s, decorated for the New York Central and the Santa Fe, arrived in stores during the fall of 1948 – in time for the holiday season. Both F3s were assigned the same engine number (2333), and the 1948 catalog proudly proclaimed the F3 to be an authentic reproduction of the giant General Motors locomotive. Ron Hollander, in *All Aboard* (Workman), tells the story of how Lionel approached the Santa Fe and the New York Central to help subsidize tooling of

"New LIONEL Super Speedliner" (1952 Lionel catalog)

the model locomotive in return for decorating the model with their road names. If so, the two railroads surely got their money's worth.

In fact, much of the success the Lionel Corporation achieved during the 1950s can be attributed to the introduction of the Santa Fe F3. This baby boomer favorite was cataloged continuously through 1966 and manufactured in huge numbers. It's fondly remembered by anyone who ever played or is familiar with a Lionel train.

Lionel's first model of the F3 was a good one. It came equipped with all the details that train enthusiasts look for, including plastic grab handles on the nose, plastic cab door ladders on both sides of the shell, a two-piece horn facing both forward and backwards on the roof, wire cloth ventilators on top of the roof, an operating knuckle coupler on the front, and metal ladders on both sides of the front and rear power trucks. Lionel truly outdid itself, creating a near-scale model in the tradition of the prewar no. 700 Hudson.

By all accounts, the F3s were tremendously successful. That esthetically pleasing nose was instantly recognizable, and the F3 fast became every boy's favorite locomotive. The catalog for 1950, Lionel's golden anniversary year, featured F3s in freight sets and offered the diesels as separate-sale items.

Good as the model was, Lionel's engineers (and eventually accountants) began making modifications to the F3's mechanism and internal configuration almost immediately. Later chapters in this book will provide an in-depth look at the changes – internal and external – the F3s underwent.

The most visible change to the exterior in 1950 came with the changing of the locomotives' numbers: the Santa Fe became 2343, and the New York Central became 2344. Also new that year were B units for both paint schemes. In terms of mechanical changes, Magne-Traction made the headlines!

The Santa Fe and the New York Central were the only F3s cataloged until the arrival of the 2345 Western Pacific in 1952. The Western Pacific didn't get much play, being shown only in profile in the "separate-sale" section of the catalog. The really big news in 1952

THE F3 AS A SCALE MODEL

The first F3 rolled off the assembly line in LaGrange, Illinois, in July of 1945 (superseding the earlier FT model). Three years later, Lionel introduced its O gauge version of the streamlined diesel with great catalog hoopla and extravagant claims about detailed accuracy: "Reproductions of the Famous General Motors Diesels." "Each is authentically striped with colorful, accurate markings." "Magnificent detail includes louvres, ladders, stanchions, panels and simulated windshield wipers." "Approximately quarter-inch scale." "Not a single detail has been left out to make this big Diesel thoroughly accurate." "Minute detail on heavy die-cast trucks."

In many respects, Lionel's F3 is a good representation of the real thing – plenty good enough for a toy train.

The Lionel model is correct for an F3 in that it has the slotted and screened dynamic brake grills on the roof directly behind the horns, rather than the round dynamic brake fan found on F7s. The Lionel model also has the F3's four carbody filters protected by louvers (instead of "chicken wire") between the two portholes (characteristic of mid-1947-and-later-production F3s).

Perhaps the oddest feature of the Lionel model is the combination chicken wire and stainless-steel filter grill running from the cab door to the rear of the unit. Early F3s had the opening covered by chicken wire; the late F3s and F7s had full-length stainless-steel grills, represented by the front and back grills of the Lionel model. No real F3 was manufactured with a combination of both.

In terms of scale dimensions, Lionel did a good job. The model measures a correct 50'-8" in length, is a scale 14'-0" high (also correct), and is only a scale 6" too narrow.

So, grills and filters are the main discrepancies between the model and the real thing. But then, as a toy train hobbyist, if you're willing to overlook the disjointed pilot and the incredible overhang on O-27 curves, grills and filters won't be problems for you.

This unit resembles an F3, but it's actually an F7. The distinctive full-length grills along the side generally indicate an F7. Burdell L. Bulgrin photo

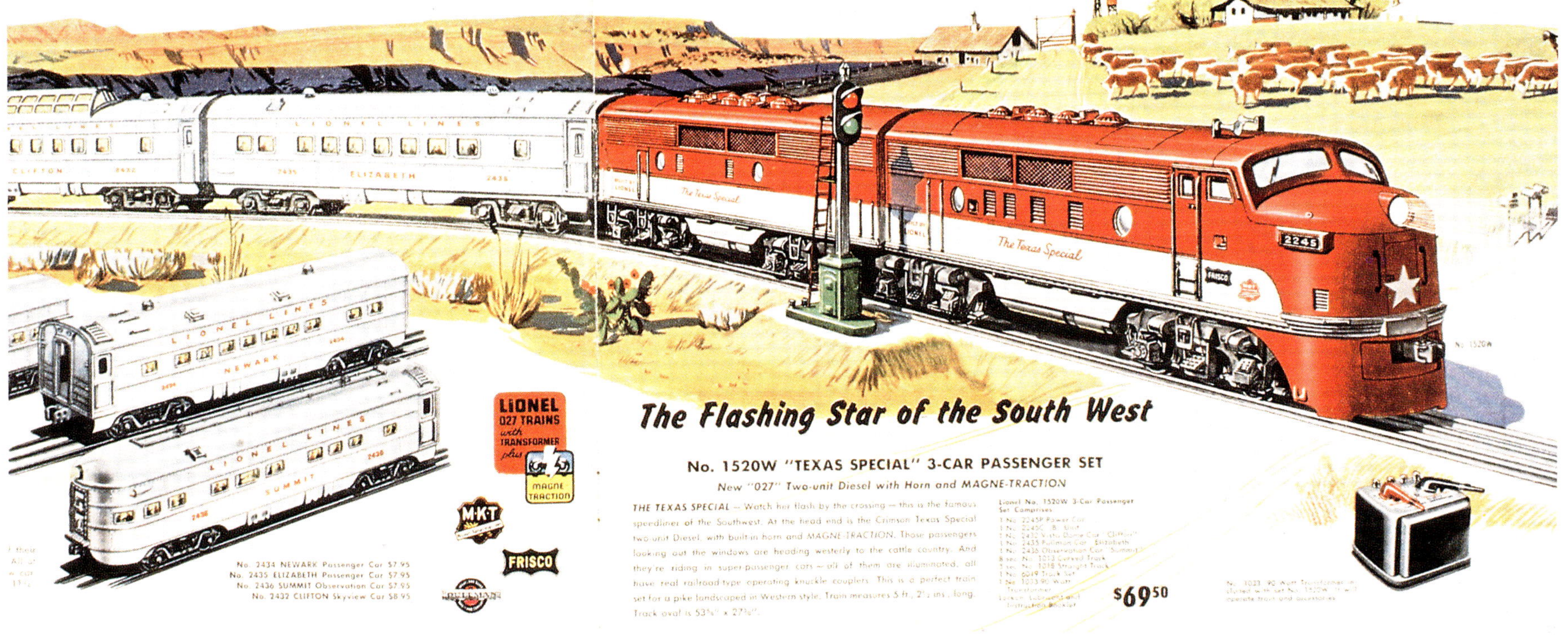

"The Flashing Star of the South West" (1954 Lionel catalog)

was the introduction of the Super Speedliner set at a whopping price of $89.50. The four "stainless steel" streamlined passenger cars were dramatically portrayed in a southwestern desert setting as well as a flat side profile of the complete set. Exciting stuff!

In 1953, the F3s' numbers changed again. But these changes only signaled more noticeable, wide-reaching changes and tell us something about the kind of thinking going on in the Lionel boardroom. The Santa Fe 2353, New York Central 2354, and Western Pacific 2355 lost their plastic grab handles and wire cloth ventilators (giving way to cast-in roof vents). This perceived reduction in quality (a polite way of saying they were "cheapened") was only the beginning of other changes in the years that followed, changes that paralleled the steady decline of the once-proud Lionel Corporation.

In 1954, the O-27 gauge 2245 *Texas Special* arrived in only an AB combination, with a single motor in the power unit. Until then, the F3s had been cataloged only as AAs, with dual motors in the power unit. The striking cardinal-and-white units were cataloged pulling both freight and passenger sets.

In just nine years, Lionel's locomotive stable went from predominantly steam to predominantly diesel, mirroring, in fact, the real railroads' shift away from steam. The 1954 catalog has a decidedly F3 flavor to it – Santa Fe, New York Central, *Texas Special,* as well as the 2356 Southern Ry., featuring the same trim (or lack of trim) as the 1953 models.

The single-motored 2243 Santa Fe in an AB combination, the dual-motored 2363 Illinois Central AB, and the 2367 "deep-sea blue" Wabash in an AB set were new for 1955. Each exhibited a "simplification" of product, as much of the remaining trim from the original design of 1948 was eliminated. It's also worth noting that an AB is intrinsically less expensive to produce than an AA, since the B unit,

"The swift, mighty Southern" (1954 Lionel catalog)

"The Sweetest Sight on Rails" (1955 Lionel catalog)

"Majestic 'O' gauge . . . from the Midwest to the East" (1956 Lionel catalog)

"Crack Super 'O' Luxury Liners" (1957 Lionel catalog)

"Thundering out of the West" (1958 Lionel catalog)

"Past gates and banjo signals streaks the New Haven" (1958 Lionel catalog)

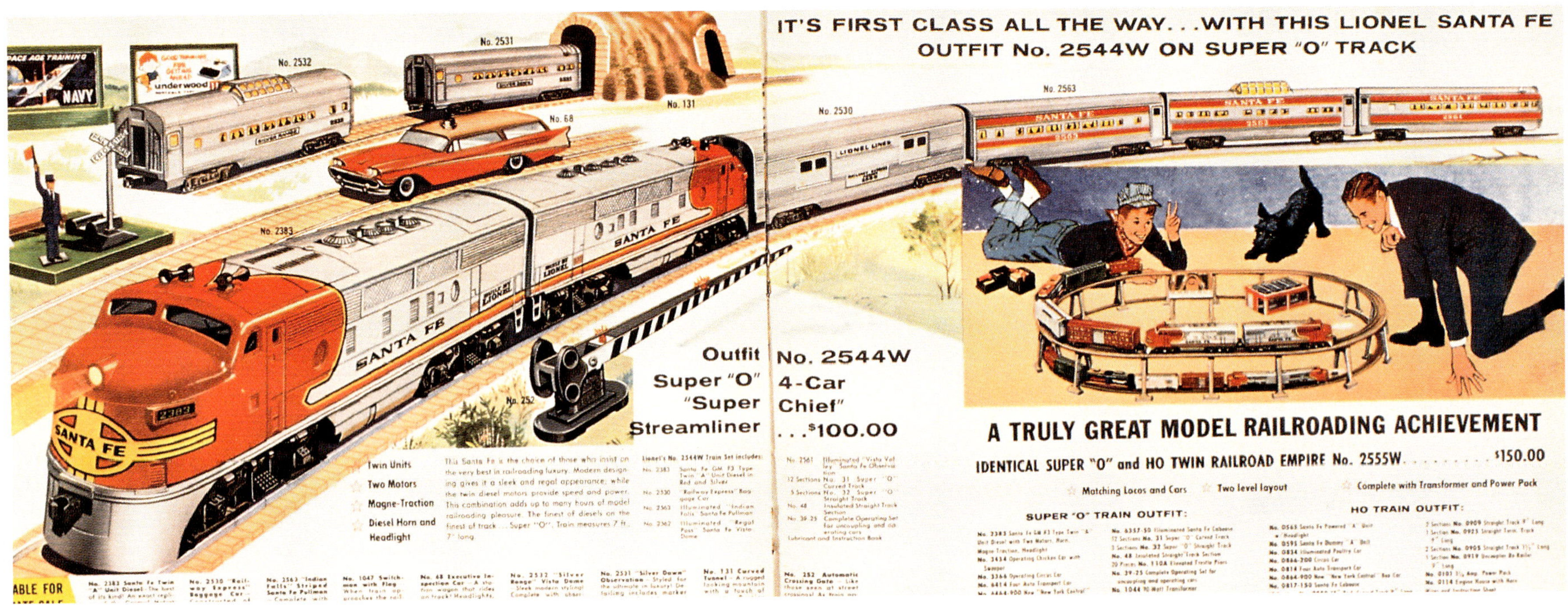

"It's First Class All the Way" (1960 Lionel catalog)

unlike the A, is a single casting with no horns, screens, portholes, windshields, or ladders to install.

The 2368 Baltimore & Ohio AB and 2378 Milwaukee Road AB introduced in 1956, together with the 2379 Canadian Pacific AA in 1957, are the most desirable and collectible of all the Lionel F3s. The dual-motored B&O 2368 and Milwaukee 2378 headed freight sets, while the dual-motored Canadian Pacific 2379 pulled passenger cars. The single-motored 2240 Wabash in an AB combination was introduced in 1956 and the dual-motored 2379 Rio Grande combination in 1957.

The 1958 consumer catalog tells us a lot about Lionel's predicament and problem-solving strategy. Apparently aware of the changing marketplace and recognizing the need to adapt to the needs and interests of its customers, Lionel introduced a line of HO scale trains (manufactured by Rivarossi and Athearn in the first two years). But it was too little, too late. Others already owned the market, and Lionel's internal situation prevented them from becoming a successful player in the growing HO market.

As far as toy trains were concerned – Lionel, American Flyer, and Marx – the boom was over. Lionel's F3 offerings in 1958 reflect this change. The single-motored 2242 New Haven combination was the only – and last – new road name cataloged by Lionel during the Postwar era. The dual-motored Santa Fe F3 returned after three years (the single-motored 2243 Santa Fe AB had been cataloged from 1955 to 1957) with a new 2383 designation.

From 1960 through 1966, the 2383 was the only F3 offered by Lionel. Although sales were down, these last sets are among the most desirable and collectible of all the F3 sets produced during the Postwar era. It's somehow fitting that the F3s began and ended with the Santa Fe – the locomotive that in the minds of most Americans is synonymous with Lionel trains.

F3 ROAD NAMES

Most of us Lionel toy train fans aren't concerned much about accuracy of detail. After all, we grew up accepting the notion that railroad tracks had three rails! If we can live with that, then why would we care if Lionel painted a locomotive in a paint scheme its real counterpart never carried? Or why would we care that the yellow stripe should have carried up over the top of the nose on the Santa Fe F3? In fact, most of us don't, but just to set the record straight, let's take a look at the road names Lionel assigned to its Postwar F3s and see how accurately they portrayed the original.

First of all, the Santa Fe had F3s, 22 four-unit locomotives (two in the blue-and-yellow freight scheme), and Lionel's paint scheme is reasonably accurate. One detail Lionel has never gotten right is the yellow stripe that should continue up over the center of the nose to the windshield. As a rule the black stripes stopped at the bottom of the headlight.

The New York Central and the Western Pacific also had F3s, and the paint schemes are close. At the time Lionel's model was produced, the light gray stripe on the passenger F3s stopped behind the second porthole of the A unit, and the B units were solid dark gray. The F3 freight units were the same, but with black instead of dark gray. Lionel seems to have used the NYC's E7 scheme as its example.

From here on out, it's kind of hit and – occasionally – miss. First, the *Texas Special* is the name of the passenger train, not the railroad or the locomotive. If Lionel had been consistent, that handsome red-and-white engine would have been called the Katy F3 or the Frisco F3. The real *Texas Special* was jointly run by the Missouri-Kansas-Texas (M-K-T, or Katy) and the St. Louis-San Francisco Ry. Each had E7 locomotives painted roughly like the Lionel versions. The top of the nose was yellow, the pilot had horizontal yellow stripes (there is a prototype like this in Lionel's archives), and the white along the side was actually stainless steel. The MKT and Frisco had F3s, but neither painted them in the *Texas Special* scheme.

The Southern Ry. had F3s, and the Lionel paint scheme is reasonably accurate.

Neither the Wabash nor the Illinois Central owned F3s.

The Baltimore & Ohio had F3s, and the paint scheme looks about right.

The Milwaukee Road had F3s – technically. They were late-production F3s (the innards or parts of the mechanism and shell were F3s) dressed up with grills and louvers characteristic of F7s. The Lionel paint scheme looks good.

Unfortunately, this handsome Bessemer F-unit was never produced. It resides in the Lionel archives.

The Canadian Pacific never had F3s, but hey, kids in Canada wanted Lionel trains too!

The Denver & Rio Grande Western had F3s – and the paint scheme is okay.

The New Haven in the orange, black, and white McGinnis paint scheme! Both the F3 and this particular paint scheme are figments of Lionel's fertile imagination!

So there you have the rundown on the road names decorating Lionel F3s. Some were on target; others missed the mark. When it comes right down to it, though, we have to recognize that marketing, accounting, and production all had their say. And they were asking questions different from those of the research and development people: What road name will sell in the Midwest and West? How can we cut costs and maximize profits? How can we speed up production?

Remember, Lionel was making toys.

LIONEL F3 PRODUCTION HISTORY: 1948–1951

Lionel's New York Central and Santa Fe F3s, both numbered 2333, from 1949.

IF YOU RECEIVED a Santa Fe or New York Central 2333 F3 diesel locomotive as a holiday gift in 1948, you probably believed it was the most wonderful present you could ever have received. It was exciting to look at, the horn and motors sounded great, and the smell – there was something magical about the smell of the ozone from those twin electric motors. How could life possibly be any better than this?

Looking back at the F3 now, five decades later and through the eyes of a somewhat more demanding adult, you could probably list a number of ways in which the model could be improved. Undoubtedly, Lionel engineers saw ways to "improve" their product even as the locomotives were rolling off the assembly line.

Of course, not all the changes Lionel made over the years were improvements; some were changes intended to save or make money, pure and simple. Whatever the reasons for the changes (some we'll

In the fall of 1949 Lionel was producing 125 F3s per hour. Photo by Al Fenn, LIFE magazine, © Time Inc.

never know), we'll describe these modifications in the upcoming pages and speculate on the reasons behind some of them.

1948

Exterior Features or Trim: First of all, let's make one thing clear: Contrary to the 1948 catalog illustration, the Santa Fe F3 was actually produced as red and silver, not red and black. All kinds of thoughts have been expressed as to how and why the catalog appears that way. Perhaps it was nothing more than an artist's failed attempt to catch the shiny, reflective look of the real locomotive's stainless-steel sheathing. Even the catalog artist, Robert Sherman, can only shrug his shoulders.

The shells for both the Santa Fe and the New York Central were molded in black plastic and then painted in the appropriate F3 colors. The lettering was rubber-stamped in black for the Santa Fe; the New York Central's was rubber-stamped in white. A red-and-white GM (General Motors) decal, which generally now is yellowed with age, was positioned above the "Built by Lionel," near the rear of both sides of the Santa Fe cab. The New York Central used a black-and-white GM decal, placed on the door panel.

Interestingly, on some Santa Fe units, GM decals were placed incorrectly on the door panels (the *Lionel Service Manual* indicated proper placement), while some New York Centrals carry the incorrect red-and-white decal – probably the result of inadequate employee training or haste. Or perhaps the proper decals simply weren't available at the time they were needed for application. The number designation, molded into the plastic number boards, was 2333 on both the Santa Fe and the New York Central.

These first models had features that would set the standard for the F3s that followed. Exterior trim included:

- Plastic grab handles on the nose (part no. 2333-16)
- Plastic cab-door ladders on both sides of the shell (2333-15)
- Two-piece horn facing both forward and rear on the roof (2332-7)
- Wire cloth ventilator on the roof (2333-12)
- Metal ladders on both sides of the front and rear power trucks (2333-57 right-hand; 2333-58 left-hand).

Perhaps the most popular feature of these early F3s was the side windows, or porthole lenses, which are often found missing today. According to the *Lionel Service Manual,* the side windows were slightly oversized and had to be forced into place with a specially shaped punch and die. Lacking that specialized equipment, one had to file the side windows to fit and then cement them into the frame. This explains why today some side windows are flat while others bulge or protrude (hence the collector term "bug-eyed" lenses). The lenses used in 1948 and 1949 were formed, then fitted to the cab. The curvature of the lens used in 1950 and 1951 was much shallower. The porthole lenses were a source of problems for several years; they were eventually abandoned, and the openings were filled in.

Interior Features (frame assembly and shell): When a Santa Fe or New York Central power-unit shell is removed, the distinguishing chassis features are the horizontally mounted motors; tubular brush holders; blue, green, and yellow wires that connect the front motor directly to the rear motor; and early-style horn assembly. Other features include a battery swivel-plate lock screw, which was blued, a process that helped prevent rusting, and a nickel-plated or blued front coupler "shield."

ARRIVAL OF THE FIRST F3s

By Lee Price

Sometime in the early summer of 1948 our boss, Jack Caffrey, was told that we would be able to take limited orders for the new F-unit sets that would be shown in the 1948 catalog, scheduled to reach the public around September 1. At the time, all we had were black-and-white glossy photos. I don't think Jack or anyone else in the Chicago office knew that the Santa Fe would appear in the catalog as red and black!

Jack was like an expectant father when he was notified that the Fs were on their way to Chicago. When the boxes arrived via Railway Express, Jack had us close the double doors to the showroom. We had a special sign, reading "Sales meeting in progress," to use when needed. I don't think I ever saw Jack so excited and animated. He lost his cool as he opened the shipment. The heavy corrugated cartons were double and heavily taped.

After removing what seemed like tons of corrugation, a New York Central AA appeared first. Jack looked it over for a moment and then rushed over to the operating display. He had all of us – myself, Reg Purnell, and Annette Borris – grabbing whatever was on the track to clear it right away.

Looking through the front door of the Lionel showroom at the Merchandise Mart in Chicago in 1947, a year before the F units arrived. Photo courtesy of Lee Price.

Jack put the locomotives on the track and shot the power to them. They lit up but didn't move. The E-unit was locked in neutral. At first he had trouble finding the lever under the locomotive, but once he found it, the locomotives took off. We heard a sound from Jack that was like a squeal of delight from a child. He said, "This beats the hell out of anything we've ever had!"

After the locomotives had made a few trips around the loop, Jack got a funny look on his face. He had been told that there would be a horn, but he couldn't get it to make a sound. Turns out the battery was inside the locomotive, wrapped in paper, and could not make contact. Before Jack had an early heart attack, Reg discovered the problem, and the locomotives, horn blowing, made several more loops.

Jack gave the controls to Reg and returned to the boxes. He was looking for the Santa Fe. You guessed it. It was in the last box he opened. We had a round glass-top table in the rear of the showroom. Before any of us got a good look at the Santa Fe, Jack quickly set it in the center of the table – without track – just set it on the table and admired it from every angle.

Then he told me to get some tools: He wanted to see the motors! I hadn't even touched our treasure, and he was telling me to decapitate it! It took only three screws, but the nose screw was not easy to get to because of the coupler skirt.

I cradled the locomotive upside down between my legs. Brain surgery would have been less nerve-wracking. When we finally got a look at the guts – two motors, horn, E-unit – we realized why it was so heavy! Jack then took the stripped locomotive to the table to see it run. And run it did!

Jack had all of us follow him to the rear office, where he made a call to J. L. Cowen himself. There were no speaker phones or conference calls in those days, but the one side of the conversation we could hear was excited and animated. We were all on a high. We had another triumph: first smoke, then milk cars, and now the F3s!

Lionel often experimented with more than one version of a part before deciding which one would be most effective. Both nickel-plated and blued front coupler shields were used during 1948 production and on into 1949. Lionel finally settled for the blued shield in later 1949 and beyond.

The underside of the power-unit shell includes some unique features as well: a blackened one-piece speed nut that secures the window shell to the cab, a blackened two-piece twin speed nut that secures the wire-cloth ventilator in position, and a large X scratched by hand on the inside of both the power and dummy unit shells (occasionally a shell is found without the X). No convincing explanation of the purpose of this X has been offered to date.

Lionel must have experimented with the truck pivot plate used with the front and rear trucks, since some early plates are made of aluminum, whereas the ones that came later are brass.

The dummy-unit frame for both the Santa Fe and the New York Central was slightly modified from the power-unit frame. On the top side, all the screw and rivet holes that secured power-unit features (among others, relay, relay bracket, horn assembly) remain open. The hole for the battery (size D) has been plugged.

1949

The 1949 production features were, for the most part, the same as those of 1948. Of course, there were minor differences as parts ran out and were replaced by slightly different versions. For example, the coupler shields on the pilot were now blued, the battery swivel-plate lock screws were not blued, and the twin speed nuts, for the last run of F3s, were not blackened.

An interesting side note: While researching the F3s, I visited the Lionel Trains Inc. showroom in Chesterfield, Michigan. On display is a production sample of a no. 2333T ("trailer" or dummy unit) dated 4-14-49. It has a nickel-plated shield, red GM decal above the "Built by Lionel," "bug-eyed" porthole lenses, and rubber-stamped lettering. Here's a 1949 piece with a shield we'd normally expect to find on F3s produced early in 1948.

Finding this dated piece made me realize that we need to be careful in assigning the words "early" and "late" to describe processes or parts when, in fact, both (or even multiple) parts or processes may have been used concurrently. Another example of transition or experimentation. This example to the contrary, blued shields predominate during 1949.

One major 1949 change concerned the way lettering was applied to the shell. Sometime during the production run, the lettering was heat-stamped rather than rubber-stamped. Today the rubber-stamped versions of the 2333 Santa Fe and New York Central are considered rare; this was not so prior to the 1970s, when these shells became prime choices for repaints. The early 1949 production shells were rubber-stamped, but after a time it became clear that heat-stamping the shells worked better and became the norm. This was a cost-effective move that involved less set-up time and, therefore, fewer labor hours.

1950

Lionel's golden anniversary year was significant for the company in many ways. The big news was the arrival of Magne-Traction and its incorporation into all Lionel locomotives, including the F3s. First offered on the no. 622 diesel switcher produced in 1949, this feature was meant to increase a locomotive's pulling power (it also helped keep the engine from careening off the track on a curve taken at high speeds).

In terms of the F3s, another big development was the introduction of B units, touted in typical advertising hyperbole as "Exact copies of the real thing."

From the point of view of the collector, however, perhaps the biggest news was that Lionel changed the numbers of its two F3s. The Magne-Traction-equipped Santa Fe changed from 2333 to 2343 and the New York Central from 2333 to 2344.

Exterior Features or Trim: In 1950, the lettering on both the Santa Fe and New York Central was heat-stamped only, and the red and white GM decal on the 2343 Santa Fe was finally placed on the door panel next to "Built by Lionel." These decals generally have also yellowed with age.

Lionel changed to a different type of plastic in 1950, which lessened the paint chipping problem. Black plastic shells were used, and for the first time, yellow-molded plastic shells were used in the production of F3s. Yellow shells were also used in 1951, and quite often as New York Central power units. One negative characteristic of Santa Fe F3s with yellow shells is that mold tends to form on the silver-painted parts unless the engines are stored in a dry environment.

The porthole lenses (2333-167) were changed to a style that didn't

THE RED-AND-BLACK F3s

This 1948 catalog art, featuring a red-and-black F unit, has puzzled Lionel fans for years. How could this have happened?

Lionel's product-development team watched what the real railroads were doing and reacted to them, producing the newest models soon after the real thing rode the rails. *Life* magazine reported in its September 5, 1949, issue that 96.7 percent of all locomotives ordered after World War II were diesels. You can bet that Lionel was aware of the dieselization of America's railroads. In 1945, Electro-Motive Division produced its first F3. Not surprisingly, Lionel offered its own version of the Santa Fe and New York Central F3s for Christmas of 1948.

What *is* surprising is that the F3s didn't grace the front cover of the 1948 consumer catalog. The F3 was, after all, a brand-new model. Did its absence from the cover suggest a lack of confidence in the new engine? Maybe it's just that the catalog cover had been designed before Lionel knew for sure the F3 would be ready. Or maybe Lionel's marketing people pushed to get the no. 671 Turbine on the cover to boost sales of that relatively uninteresting model. Perhaps J. L. Cowen's known preference for steam locomotives made a diesel on the cover politically risky until the F3 proved itself. Or maybe marketing felt the flashy new diesel locomotives would sell themselves and didn't need a catalog cover – "Give 'em the center spread [where the catalog naturally opens] instead." We'll never know for sure.

And how about the unusual artwork? The drawing doesn't really capture the shape of the real locomotive. The artist *must* have been able to see the real thing; after all, the New York Central main line isn't all that far from Lionel's plant or showroom. Perhaps we can excuse the artist for his inability to draw the shape properly, but how can we excuse him for the black-and-red paint scheme on the Santa Fe unit?

Bob Sherman, famous Lionel catalog artist of the 1940s and '50s, was interviewed by Bill Curtis in the February 1992 issue of *Classic Toy Trains* magazine. Bob sheds a little light on the mystery. Here's what he had to say about the F3 and the 1948 catalog.

Bill: What kinds of models were you given to draw from?

Bob: Usually they were hand-built and hand-painted models, and I'd draw what I was given. When they were bringing out the F3 diesel, however, they had nothing. They told me to go to a model store and buy a scale model kit* for an F3 engine. I had a week to build it, paint it, and draw it. So the first year of the F3, I drew from the model I built.

Bill: That would certainly explain the odd, non-Lionel contours in the 1948 catalog, but what about the red-and-black Santa Fe paint scheme?

Bob: I don't know how that came about. I drew it, but I had nothing to do with selecting the colors. Leo Mayer was my boss. I was working for him. They must have told him that the Santa Fe engine was red and black instead of red and silver. Where those colors came from, I just don't know.

*Perhaps the model Bob bought was an HO scale Varney die-cast F3. That model was announced in an ad in the December 1947 issue of *Model Railroader* magazine and would have been available about the time Bob was working on the catalog. Varney was the largest HO model producer of the time and their models would have been widely available. The problem is, the odd headlight and unique grill and vent patterns on the Lionel F3 don't match the Varney model; neither do they match any other model we're aware of or the real F3! The mystery remains.

NYC F3 from 1950 (2344 and 2344T) with individual boxes and master carton. Note the missing porthole lens on the rear unit.

protrude like the earlier ones. The new design didn't keep the lenses in their openings any better and are often missing from 1950 models found today (a problem Lionel would finally solve in 1952).

Interior Features (frame assembly and shell): In 1950, engineers redesigned the horn assembly and attached it to the sides of the power-frame assembly. The frame itself was left unchanged, and the two screw holes where the 1948/1949 horn assembly was attached at the rear were left unfilled. These frames continued through 1950–1951 until the supply was exhausted; then the holes were filled, leaving only impressions in subsequent frames.

In 1950, the frame for the dummy A unit was modified, as the slot where the E-unit lever protruded was filled in; this is not noticeable on the outside of the frame. On the inside, however, the slot is visible, but is now grooved.

The tubular brush holders of the original design were replaced by a redesigned hairpin-type (*Lionel Service Manual* 12/58). It's interesting to note, and a point to keep in mind when trying to date changes, that *Lionel Service Manual* pages were often produced at a much later date than the changes themselves and were sometimes incorrect. However, this 12/58 entry is right on the money.

For some reason, perhaps relating to cost, the locomotive's connector wiring was changed to black, replacing the three color-coded wires used during 1948 and 1949 production. The top of the E-unit changed slightly, as well, and the protective tape was no longer used. Engineers made one simple improvement when they slotted the screw that held the battery swivel-plate in place; now you could use a screwdriver to back it out, though the screw was still knurled for removal by hand.

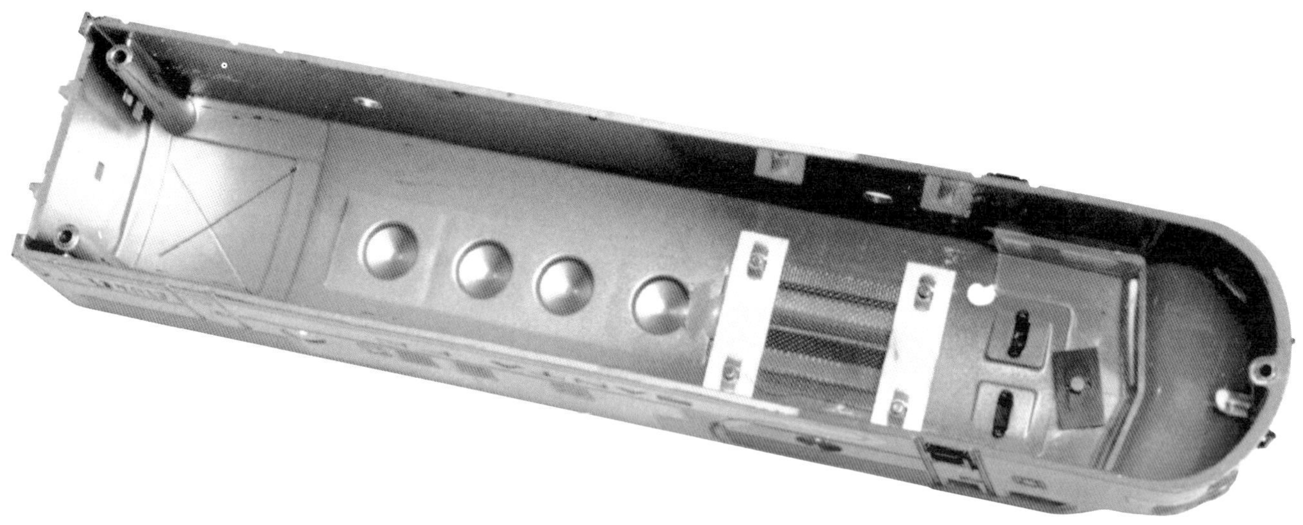

Clues for dating this shell include the scribed X (pre-1951), chrome twin speed nuts (1949/50), and blackened single speed nut (1948/50). Don't forget to consider "transition."

During the 1950 production year, the speed nut and the twin speed nut became shiny and were no longer blackened, although a transition of parts still occurred. Finally, sometime during 1950 the decision was made to stop scratching the X on the inside of the body shell; whatever purpose it had served was no longer required.

The brand-new B units were rubber-stamped 2343C (Santa Fe) or 2344C (NYC) on the underside of the frame. Just like the A units, the B units came supplied with wire cloth ventilators. Some 1950-production (and later) Santa Fe and New York Central B units exist without appropriate numbers rubber-stamped on them.

A couple of intriguing thoughts relating to the 1950 catalog. A small, loose sketch of the Santa Fe warbonnet was one of four elements on the catalog's front cover. The suggestion seems to be that the cars behind it are silver. Could Lionel have matching passenger cars in mind at this point, or was this an example of artistic license? Look also at the photo of the B units on page 26 of the catalog. Silver passenger cars?

From left, blued lock screw (1948/1949), lock screw (1949/1950), not blued but with slot (1950–1955), and rounded with slot (1955–1966).

1951

Lionel had experienced an outstanding production year in 1950 and had every reason to be optimistic about 1951 – except for the news from Korea. In June of 1950, North Korea invaded South Korea, and President Harry Truman sent American troops abroad once again. The news of fighting on the Korean peninsula must have brought back memories of shutting down the toy train lines and retooling for wartime production only a decade earlier.

Concerns about whether history would repeat itself must have been discussed in the Lionel boardroom. Undoubtedly contingency plans were laid out and strategies determined. Could the strategy selected have been the conservative one in which only 13 sets would be offered in 1951? Or were there other factors that limited the company's offering?

As a result of the "police action" and perceived inflationary pressures, the government created, in 1951, the Office of Price Stabilization (OPS). The purpose of this agency was to establish price controls that would help to maintain economic stability. The impact on industry (including Lionel) was to create uncertainty and a lot of paperwork. However, by 1953 the police action in Korea was over, controls were removed, and the OPS was abolished. Lionel was once again able to focus its attention on toy train production.

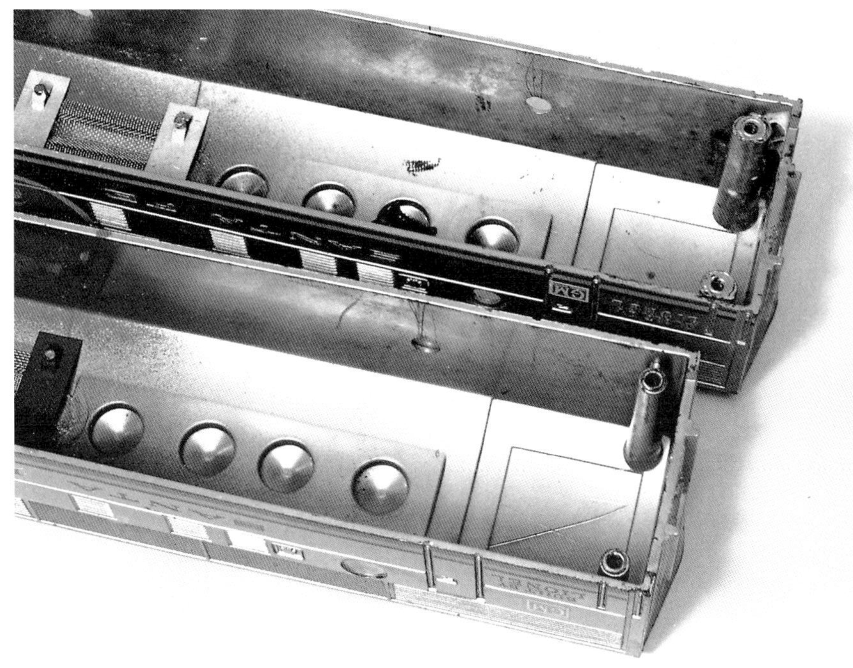

In 1951, the mounting bosses (posts at end of shell) became thicker, and the mysterious scribed X disappeared.

Lionel's net sales for 1951 (fiscal year ending February 29, 1952) were about $19 million, just under 2.5 million less than 1950 – not too bad considering the role government was taking in product pricing and the possibility of another world war looming over them. The numbers raise an interesting question, however. In 1950, Lionel cataloged 22 sets; in 1951, only 13. How could Lionel catalog nine fewer sets in 1951 and still manage to produce comparable net sales? (It should be noted that income from wartime contracts may have been included in the sales figures.)

Perhaps Lionel simply produced a smaller variety of items, though in greater quantities. This makes sense in terms of efficiency. If Lionel cut back on the number of sets they were offering, that would mean they could reduce the number of different cars and locomotives they needed to produce. That, in turn, would mean saving on tear-down time as well as set-up time in the injection machines, the paint booths, the assembly line, etc., to say nothing of employee training. It's certainly more efficient to change an operation less often and to keep the lines moving longer with single products.

Lionel boxes may be able to shed some light on this issue. Until recently, train boxes have been pretty much ignored by collectors; now, however, boxes have taken on a collectibility of their own. This means that more and more boxes are coming to light. Interestingly enough, we're able to learn a lot about the history of toy train production from the boxes that items were packaged in. For instance, by looking at Santa Fe set 2175W from 1951, we learn that Lionel used more than one vendor to produce both individual and set boxes. Prior to 1951 Lionel generally used a single vendor to produce F3 boxes.

We can draw some conclusions about production numbers based on the relative number of boxes available on the collector market. At present there appears to be an abundance of set 2175W boxes from 1951 as compared to 2175W from 1950. Remember, there were two Santa Fe sets offered for sale in 1950, but only one in 1951. This would seem to support the hypothesis that in 1951 Lionel increased the number of set unit sales while decreasing the total number of sets available.

In support of this conclusion is the observation that there appears to be a lot more Santa Fe and New York Central F3s available on the collector market with 1951 pickup rollers than with 1950-style rollers.

Exterior Features or Trim: The 1951 shells are the same as those of 1950 production, although the GM decals generally appear to have stayed brighter.

Interior Features (frame assembly and shell): The easiest way to tell the difference between a 1951 F3 and a 1950 model is to examine the roller pickups. In 1951, Lionel changed from the larger 622-138 type to the smaller 2343-95 type. On the inside of the shell, the two rear support columns (mounting bosses), where the shell is screwed to the frame, were made noticeably larger. This change was actually made near the end of the 1950 production year, about the time the mysterious X disappeared.

The trucks on the dummy A unit were redesigned, and the "Lionel Corporation" nameplate and truck pivot plate were removed. The 1951 B unit was physically the same as the 1950 unit, although Lionel increased the price from $11.95 to $13.75; OPS stickers exist for both units.

In 1951, Lionel sent dealers OPS packets that contained a predetermined number of stickers to be placed on sets and separate-sale items. In 1952, OPS information was printed on the box. You may

DUAL MOTORS AND CLEAR BODY

By Lee Price

The most collectible of all F3s: the clear body.

We had six or eight AA New York Central and Santa Fe F3s. Jack [Caffrey, Lionel's head of sales in Chicago] called his direct buyers and distributors for a "presentation" meeting in our offices [at the Merchandise Mart] the next week. He had a very limited allocation of the units for his ten-state area, and so he tried to spread the stock evenly. We kept one locomotive on display without the body so everyone could see the two motors. Almost every store did the same when deliveries were made late in October through Christmas of 1948.

It was not until the Toy Fair in March of 1949 that clear body units were made. We had a total delivery of 10 or 12. All were Santa Fe. I don't think any New York Central clear-body units were made.

I don't believe that more than 100 clear-body units were made in all. A few of them were given to our large jobbers like General Electric Supply and Gray-Bar Electric. And some of them may have been returned to New York for destruction. Of course, these units were never made with collectors in mind.

LIONEL'S NEW GENERAL MOTORS F3 DIESEL WHIZZES PAST AN OLDER MODIFIED PRAIRIE MODEL IN WHICH A WORKMAN DROPS A PILL THAT MAKES REAL SMOKE

LIONEL DIESELIZES

An old railroad company brings miniature locomotives up to date

CONTINUED ON NEXT PAGE 67

A *Life* magazine article referred to 1948 production problems caused by a diesel horn that "failed to blow true." Photo by Al Fenn, LIFE magazine, © Time Inc., reprinted with permission.

REAL LIFE DEEP-TONED HORN

An intriguing detail about production of the F units is revealed in the September 5, 1949, issue of *Life* magazine. The writer mentions that Lionel's 1948 program was "halted" by a diesel horn that failed to "blow true." One might legitimately ask if the problem was ever solved! However, assuming the typical F3 horn sound is the desired sound, it's interesting to speculate about the source of the failure to "blow true."

No mention of horn problems shows up in the *Lionel Service Manual.* And Lee Price, Lionel employee at the Chicago office, makes no mention (in his accompanying sidebars) of horn problems. Quite the contrary. According to Price, the crew in the Chicago office soon had the horn blowing noisily as the locomotive raced around their company display layout.

Furthermore, a Madison Hardware advertisement in the February/March 1949 *Model Builder* explained that the new Lionel F3s contained a realistic "Diesel-pitched horn." No mention of a problem. The ad, along with the 1948 catalog copy, incorrectly states that the horn was in the dummy unit instead of the power unit. Apparently, the catalog and the ad were printed before F3 production was under way. It seems likely that the erroneous descriptions reveal Lionel's original intention – to put the horn and battery in the dummy A unit.

The 1949 catalog straightens the record. "This [powered] unit also contains authentic, deep-pitched Diesel Horn – rubber cushion mounted – which blows by remote control. The reference to "rubber cushion mounted" is interesting; was this an attempted solution to the problem of a horn that failed to "blow true"?

Apparently, whatever problem Lionel perceived in the horn was solved by 1950 as the catalog makes only routine mention of the "Real life deep-toned horn."

Set 2175W with Santa Fe F3 AA from 1951. Note the wartime OPS sticker in the upper left corner of the set box.

notice that OPS stickers are often found on F3 set boxes, but never on individual F3 boxes. The reason for this is that in 1951, the Santa Fe and the New York Central were not offered for separate sale in the consumer catalog. There were no master cartons, and the filled individual F3 boxes were just placed inside the set box.

The bottom master carton for 2343 AA F3s is from 1950; the top one is from 1952 (note printed OPS). In 1951 the F units were not offered for separate sale, hence no master cartons.

LIONEL F3 PRODUCTION HISTORY: 1952–1954

Joining the Santa Fe and New York Central F3s during this period were the Western Pacific (1952), *Texas Special* (1954), and Southern (1954).

1952

LIONEL'S ANNUAL REPORT for 1952 (year ended February 28, 1953) reported a shareholder-pleasing improvement over the prior year. Net sales were up more than $9 million – a 47.5 percent increase over 1951 – to $28,159,463. Not all of that was train sales, however. Those record-breaking numbers included, for the first time, sales from Lionel's wholly owned subsidiaries, Airex Corporation and Airex Manufacturing Company, Inc. In addition, Lionel was producing material for the military, though, according to Lionel President Lawrence Cowen, government work was "not highly profitable." Nevertheless, Lionel's annual report to stockholders suggested that both the present and future would be profitable and that the company was more than prepared to react to any changes in the economy.

KOREAN WAR OUTBREAK

The OPS (Office of Price Stabilization) was created as a result of the Korean War. For a time, OPS stickers went on Lionel boxes; eventually the boxes were printed with OPS information on them.

Lionel had been celebrating its golden anniversary for only a few months when war broke out in Korea. On June 25, 1950, Communist-ruled North Korea attacked South Korea in an effort to unify the divided country by force. The United Nations responded by sending a multinational force (including Americans) to drive back the invaders. For almost 3 years, America was embroiled in the conflict until an armistice was signed on July 27, 1953.

Not much has been said about the impact of the Korean War on Lionel's toy train production. Unlike World War II, when toy train production was canceled by the government, this time toy trains continued to roll off the assembly lines. Undoubtedly there were shortages of some materials, including those used in producing Magne-Traction, and we know that Lionel had defense contracts. We also know that the Office of Price Stabilization was established during this period, at least in part as a result of the war. Some interesting comments relating to wartime production can be found in Lionel's annual reports from the period. The first annual message published after the start of the war reported on the fiscal year ending February 28, 1951. Lionel president Lawrence Cowen noted that managers met in October of 1950 and closely examined the 1950 product line. They declared it to be "outstandingly the most advanced and attractive group of trains and accessories ever offered to the public." He went on to say, "Therefore, it was decided to effect as few changes as possible between our 1950 and 1951 lines." Interesting comment.

Cowen earlier touched on the real reason for limiting changes: "We were thoroughly aware that in a short time the facilities of our Engineering Department would be largely devoted to defense work and would, therefore, be unable to apply its energies to development of our normal civilian products."

In reference to Airex, Lionel's subsidiary producer of fishing tackle, Cowen observed that "They, of course, are also subject to limiting orders regarding the use of materials." Note the use of the word "also."

In the 1952 annual report (fiscal year ending February 29, 1952), Cowen noted that the train business was flourishing. "The demand for Lionel trains and accessories has far exceeded our original planning for 1952–1953. Therefore, we have revised production to accommodate this increased volume of business, and *materials being available* [author's italics] it is our present intention to fill these orders in their entirety." He added, "Production is proceeding according to schedule, and materials, fortunately, have been available."

The consumer catalogs could serve as another indicator of the limited impact the war had on toy train production. For comparison purposes, we should look at 1949 production. In its consumer catalog, Lionel offered 26 sets. In 1950, Lionel offered 22 sets: four were F3 sets; two included the no. 773 Hudson, two included the new Alco (one freight and one passenger), and one was led by the new 2330 GG1 with dual motors. This is not the production of a company whose hands were tied by the war, and the annual reports attest to the company's success.

However, Lionel had experienced war twice before; both were world wars, and managers knew what that meant in terms of toy trains. Would the Korean invasion turn out to be World War III? Nobody knew for sure. One can almost hear the concern in Cowen's words of May 14, 1951: "It is extremely difficult to forecast business for 1951. All manufacturers are keenly aware that world conditions are a vital factor in any future plans."

During 1952 Lionel produced four more cataloged sets than they had in 1951. In addition to two Santa Fe freight sets (two were also cataloged in 1951), Lionel cataloged a Santa Fe passenger set for the very first time. This set, no. 2190W, included Lionel's brand-new line of aluminum-style passenger cars that rivaled those of their competitor, American Model Toys.

Lionel also increased the number of available F3s by adding the 2345 Western Pacific to the product line. The new Western Pacific was offered for separate sale only.

Exterior Features or Trim (shell and trucks): In 1952, Lionel began to paint and decorate their F3s using gray plastic shells. Rather than remove the shell or scratch the paint to determine the color of the molded plastic, simply look at the outside of the cabs. In 1952, F3s used the newer snap-in porthole window (2343-133) and the smaller black-and-white GM decal. However, keep in mind the transition principle; Lionel experimented by using these same new features on some late 1951 models of the Santa Fe. As a defining characteristic, then, look for the gray shell. Some 1952 New York Central nose decals have an orangish appearance, and Santa Fe nose decals are somewhat different as well. The "S" in Santa Fe is noticeably different, looking more like a backwards "Z." The same style decal shows up again in the 1960s.

Interior Features (frame assembly and shell): Distinguishing between 1951 and 1952 production is difficult in this regard, except for a couple of changes made late in the run when the Western Pacifics were being assembled. To this point, the "realistic diesel horn" had been manufactured by the Delta Electric Company of Marion, Indiana. The manufacturer's name and location were stamped on the top of the horn. Some Western Pacifics, however, show up with a similar horn, but without the manufacturer's name on top and with the Lionel Corporation's name and location stamped on the bottom. Also, the tabs that hold the battery cover in place face upwards instead of down.

Finally, another change that could easily go unnoticed was the lengthening of the two rear mounting screws used for the Western Pacifics. (It's possible the longer screws could have been used on Santa Fe and New York Central models as well. I've examined only one verifiable Santa Fe.) The new screws are 9/16" long pan-head type; the shorter ones are 1/2" flathead.

1953

The F3s produced in 1953 are the same three road names as those produced in 1952. Lionel made no dramatic changes in the way of

The Santa Fe nose herald underwent changes during its Postwar lifetime (from left): 2343 (1950), bold vertical black stripes and regular S; 2343 (1952), bold vertical black stripes and "backwards Z" S on Santa Fe; 2343 (1952), narrow vertical black stripes and backwards Z; and 2383 (1964), narrow black stripes and backwards Z.

AMT BEATS LIONEL TO THE STREAMLINED PUNCH

By Roger Carp

AMT's passenger cars looked good behind Lionel's Santa Fe F3s.

Almost as soon as Lionel decided to develop models of the F3 diesel, designers and salesmen must have given thought to bringing out matching passenger cars. The 1950 catalog cover hints at silver cars behind the warbonnet locomotives; behind the B unit on page 26 in the 1950 catalog are what appear to be silver heavyweight passenger cars; and original silver-and-red heavyweights have been reported on in *Classic Toy Trains* magazine. Lionel also offered silver versions of their O-27 gauge 2400-series cars before the streamlined aluminum cars in the 2530 series made their debut in 1952.

To Lionel's chagrin, however, the bright and shiny O gauge Pullmans, Vista-Dome, and observation car that made up the Super Streamliner set weren't the first streamlined aluminum cars on the market. An upstart firm based in Auburn, Indiana, had introduced gorgeous passenger cars in 1948. American Model Toys marketed a pair of Lionel-compatible sand-cast Pullman coaches and an observation car painted and lettered for the New York Central or the Pennsylvania RR.

AMT began using extruded aluminum in 1949 to lower its costs, increase production, and make its models more compatible with Lionel's F3s. By 1950, AMT had eight passenger cars: mail express car, diner, bedroom-roomette Pullman, Vista-Dome, observation, day coach, crew or combination car, and baggage car. Each car came lettered for the New York Central or the Santa Fe and looked great with Lionel's F3s.

The AMT streamliners captured part of the O gauge market for three reasons. First, they were realistic models of contemporary passenger equipment, exactly what many consumers wanted. Second, these cars boasted a style all their own, including near-scale length, interior illumination, metal nameplates, prototypical window patterns, and accurate drumheads. Third and most obvious, they filled a gap in the market thus far neglected by Lionel.

When Lionel came out with its own streamliners in 1952, AMT struggled to make its cars more appealing by offering streamliners lettered for the Pennsylvania RR (*Broadway Limited*) and Southern Ry. (*Crescent Limited*) in 1952. A year later, AMT advertised models of the *400* on the Chicago & North Western and the *Texas Special* on the Missouri-Kansas-Texas and the St. Louis-San Francisco.

Unfortunately, neither these new trains nor AMT's new near-scale models of freight cars and diesels were enough to overtake Lionel, and sales declined in 1953. In the fall of 1954, Kusan, a Nashville-based toy company, bought the AMT line.

Lionel entered the market late, but they were not the loser.

It was 1952 before Lionel streamlined their fleet. This is set 2190W.

From 1948 through 1952 the locomotive numbers are molded *into* the plastic marker lens (2333 and 2343), but from 1953 through 1966 the numbers are *raised* (2243, 2353, and 2383).

paint schemes or redesigns. What 1953 is notable for is the beginning of the "cheapening" process. The market was changing, and Lionel was trying to respond.

Exterior Features or Trim (shell and trucks): In 1953, Lionel changed the numbers of all three F3s. The 2343 Santa Fe became 2353, the 2344 New York Central 2354, and the 2345 Western Pacific 2355. The numbers on the number board were in relief rather than molded into the plastic as before.

Although the 1953 consumer catalog still showed the Santa Fe with a red-and-white GM decal, the symbol was now heat-stamped in black onto the door panel next to the "Built by Lionel" on both sides of the cab. This was the case on all three F3s produced.

Lionel, like any company then or now, was constantly looking for ways to increase productivity and decrease costs. By this point, the F units were firmly established as part of the line; thousands had been produced. They were a proven product with most of the bugs removed. Now it was time to start adjusting, modifying, and economizing. For example, the plastic grab handles were eliminated (extra material costs, additional step in the assembly process, breakage) and the wire cloth ventilators were replaced by roof vents that became part of the casting (same reasons as above). These changes – and others that followed – helped reduce production and material costs, but in retrospect, they also marked the beginning of the end for Lionel, spiraling down to the Lionel Corporation's dissolution and sale in 1969.

Interior Features (frame assembly and shell): Starting in 1953, the lamp bracket and holder became part of the casting, and at the rear of the cab, the two screws that secured the cab to the frame were replaced by a two-prong bracket, eliminating the need for the two rear columns (mounting bosses). The clear-plastic windshield assembly was glued to the roof on the inside of the F3 shell, eliminating the need for a speed nut.

The complete horn assembly, which until now had been located in the power A unit, was moved to the dummy A unit. The horn itself was the same as the one used in the 2345 from 1952, but the horn bracket was shorter. In addition, the horn was moved slightly forward on the dummy A frame, creating the need for two additional screw holes. This allowed the shell to be removed from the chassis. During 1954 production, the new screw holes are visible, but the previous holes were filled in and only impressions were left.

With the removal of the horn relay bracket, the power A unit was no longer crowded, and the E-unit became easier to service. The connecting wires were no longer secured on top of the relay bracket by a single rubber band, which, incidentally, is usually

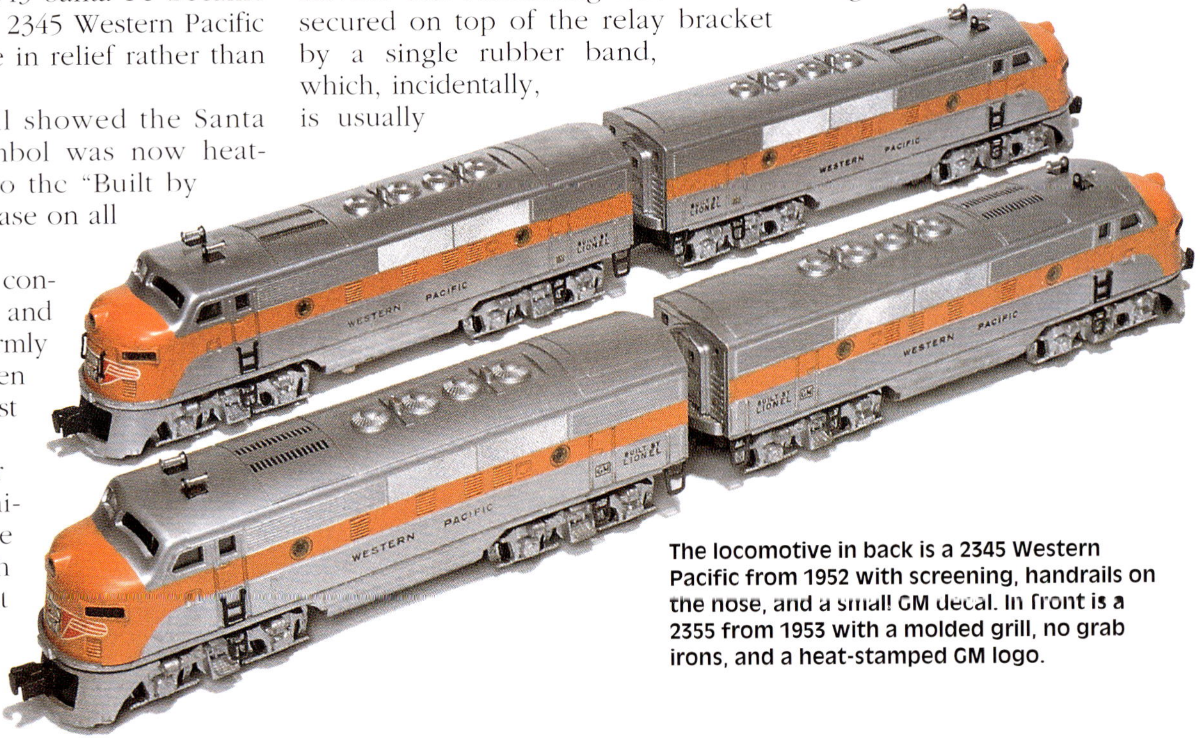

The locomotive in back is a 2345 Western Pacific from 1952 with screening, handrails on the nose, and a small GM decal. In front is a 2355 from 1953 with a molded grill, no grab irons, and a heat-stamped GM logo.

Texas Special AB units pulled two sets in 1954: (left) 1520W passenger and (right) 1517W freight. The packaging is typical of 1954.

missing. The power A unit still showed the holes where the horn bracket was secured to the frame on the pre-1953 line.

Not surprisingly, the B unit also lost its wire cloth ventilator in 1953. The way the shell was secured to the frame also changed. Prior to 1953, the shell was secured by four screws, one on the bottom at each corner of the frame. However, in 1953, the frame was redesigned so that only a single screw at each end of the shell was needed. The holes where the four screws would have gone were still there, but in 1955 these were filled in and only impressions were left.

1954

Is it unreasonable to assume that in selecting the next F3 road name to offer, Lionel looked at where their previous success had been? "Western Pacific? A California railroad mostly – pretty local. Not a smashing success. Paint's not real durable and the decals aren't holding up well. Time to drop it from the line. New York Central? Big center of population, sales okay, but not a real flashy color scheme. Lacks pizzazz. Santa Fe? California to Chicago, the romantic Old West. [Remember, westerns were among the most popular TV shows and movies at the time.] And don't forget that eye-catching red paint scheme. Our best seller."

"Let's stick with red and the western connection! Maybe the Missouri-Kansas-Texas ('Katy') should be next. How about 'The Flashing Star of the South West,' the *Texas Special*?"

The bright red and brilliant white 2245 *Texas*

The handsome 2356 Southern F3 AA from 1954.

From left: Western Pacific 2355 (1953) with no roof dimple, 2245 *Texas Special* (1954) with dimple behind grills (interestingly, painted over a Santa Fe warbonnet), and 2373 Canadian Pacific (1957) with dimple and grill starting to fill in.

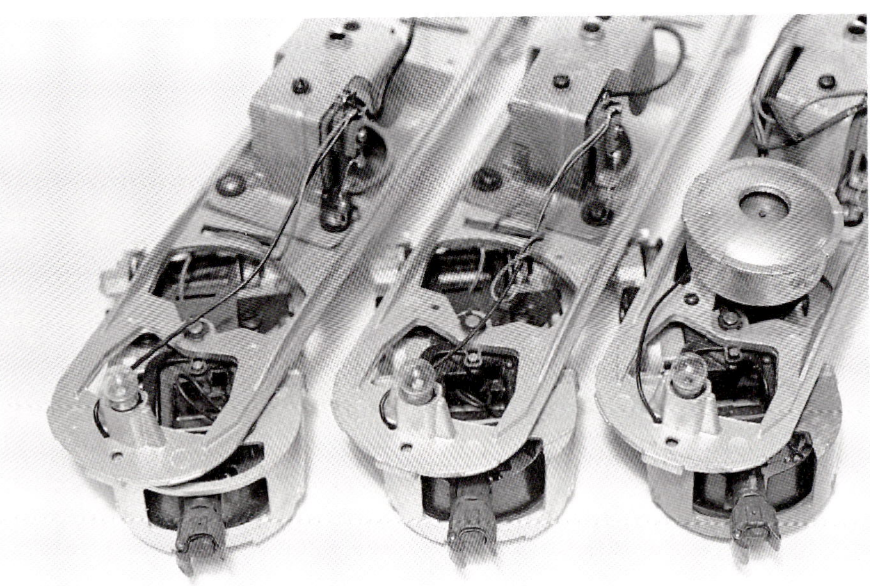

The power units shown here are from 1953 and 1954. The pilots illustrate the production history. From left: 1953, bar over coupler, notched pilot bottom, and no holes for horn bracket; 1954, no bar, still notched, and holes for horn bracket (left front and right rear of second opening over truck); 1954, bar gone, notch removed, and horn installed.

Special made its debut in 1954 as part of two O-27 sets: a freight and a passenger. This approach represented a new marketing strategy. By putting the single-motor F units in O-27 sets, Lionel was cutting costs while still appealing to a different market and, with a lower sales price, increasing volume.

The *Texas Special* was produced in a new AB combination, instead of AA, and carried a single motor, instead of double. Both changes were benefits for the cost-conscious Lionel Corporation.

"How about other regions of the country? What market have we missed?"

The 2356 Southern Ry. was cataloged as an ABA unit in set 2231W, selling for $79.50. When sold separately, the AA combination retailed for $47.50, while the 2356C B unit cost $9.95.

Exterior Features (on shell and trucks): The shell used in 1954 was the same as the one used in 1953. However, early in the production year a round dimple began to appear on the shell directly behind the roof vents. The mark is a leftover from the injection-molding process, as the dimple helps hide the sink mark usually seen at the sprue location. When plastic is injected into a mold, it passes through a "gate," or opening, and then spreads throughout the mold. This mark is at the point of the gate in the mold. From 1955 on, the last roof vent becomes partially filled in. In late 1953, or early 1954 (about the same time as the roof dimple appeared), the part number for the side window changed from 2343-133 to 2353-11. The difference appeared to be in the way the windows were staked.

Interior Features (frame assembly and shell): Until 1954, assembly of the coupler and drawbar, complete with pilot and shield, was difficult and time-consuming. The difficulty was caused by the bar that went across the top of the metal pilot casting. In late 1953, Lionel experimented by removing the top bar from the pilot casting of some F3s. Although examples with the top bar were still being produced in 1953, Lionel eliminated the top bar during 1954. This change eased coupler assembly and service.

Also with regard to the pilot, from the very beginning, the pilot

An interesting clue in determining the date of an F3. The coupler knuckle on the left features an embossed circle, indicating pre-1954 production. The one on the right features rectangular embossing, suggesting 1954 or later production.

was notched in the center, most likely to prevent the engine from shorting out when passing over uneven trackwork or switches. In 1954, Lionel finally evened out the bottom of the pilot by grinding off the low-hanging outside portions of the pilot to the same level as the bottom of the notch. To see this, turn an F3 unit from 1954 or later upside down and inspect the uneven cuts across the bottom of the pilot.

The introduction of the *Texas Special* as a single-motor AB, instead of a double-motor AA, meant that the horn assembly had to be returned to the powered A unit. However, the horn bracket was too short to clear the rear-mounted motor of the *Texas Special*. Lionel solved this problem by placing the horn in the area left vacant by the removal of the front motor. Two additional screw holes were cored and tapped, and the horn was secured.

Once the frame was modified, the two screw holes were visible from the inside, but not always from the outside. Lionel also used some two-prong brackets that are olive-colored instead of the usual black. In 1954, the top of the F3 coupler knuckle was engraved, whereas in prior years the knuckle simply had a round indentation. This change helps distinguish 1954 production from 1953.

With regard to the B units, the mounting screws were usually cadmium-plated instead of blackened, and the bottom of the frame had 2356C stamped in silver or 2245C stamped in black, with few exceptions noted.

Lionel F3 Production History: 1955–1957

New paint schemes introduced between 1955 and 1957 include (right to left): Illinois Central (1955), Wabash (1956), Baltimore & Ohio (1956), Milwaukee Road (1956), Canadian Pacific (1957), and Denver & Rio Grande Western (1957).

1955

IN THE EARLY 1900s, Lionel did its part to help win the Great War. Then in the 1940s, Lionel retooled and produced materials to help win World War II. Finally, in the early 1950s, the Korean War created its own problems for the toy train manufacturer. But in 1955, Lionel found itself in a new kind of war – a war for the hearts and minds of young boys, young engineers, Lionel's customers. Who or what was the enemy? Television for starters. Walt Disney's *Davy*

Crockett was a big summer phenomenon (the three-part series had aired on the *Disneyland* television program in December 1954, January 1955, and February 1955), and the movie version was released to theaters in the summer of 1955. Only a few years earlier, every boy had wanted to be a Lionel engineer, but by late 1955 every youngster wanted to be Davy Crockett and to wear a coonskin cap.

And that was only the beginning. Rock and roll was here to stay with classics such as "Rock around the Clock," by Bill Haley and His Comets, spending eight weeks at number one on the charts. At the other end of the spectrum were crooners like Pat Boone or groups like the Platters. And only a year later, the King – Elvis Presley – would come to claim his throne. Times were changing; boys of the late 1940s and early '50s were growing up and moving on to other interests: rock and roll, girls, and Chevys (not necessarily in that order). Whether Lionel knew it or not, toy trains were in trouble.

Nevertheless, 1955 proved to be a favorable year as net sales totalled $20,512,285, with a net income of $1,178,554. "Dividends Per Share" and "Net Income To Sales" were the same as the previous two years.

Lionel added two more dual-motor diesels to their line, with the introduction of the 2363 Illinois Central and the 2367 Wabash – two midwestern lines. However, in another marketing – or cost-saving – move, the dual-motored F3s were produced in AB combinations, instead of the usual AA. Although the 2353 Santa Fe, 2354 New York Central, and 2356 Southern were still listed for separate sale, they undoubtedly represented leftover 1954 inventory. The single-motored 2243 Santa Fe was introduced, in an AB combination, in an effort to increase diesel sales in the O-27 line.

Exterior Features or Trim (shell and trucks): In 1955, the shell was modified as the side windows and door ladders became part of the casting. The ornamental horn also changed as it became a one-piece unit. The metal ladders on the sideframes were eliminated, as was the pilot shield, just two more details removed in the cheapening process.

One of the easiest 1955 changes to spot is the knuckle pin on the operating couplers. Many of the F3s produced have a shiny knuckle pin, instead of the blackened version that had been the standard in previous years.

Interior Features (frame assembly and shell): In 1955, the frame underwent a major redesign to include vertically mounted motors instead of horizontal and magnetic couplers instead of coil wound. The redesigned frame was marked no. 2243-38 instead of 2333-20. This new part number distinguishes the change.

Having removed the pilot shield, Lionel engineers redesigned the pilot itself, getting rid of the gaping hole by making the coupler opening smaller. Also redesigned were the power and dummy trucks for both the double- and single-motored F3s. Instead of the previous style

The 2363 Illinois Central AB set (with master carton and individual boxes) from 1955.

that featured a double pickup, the redesigned power truck for dual-motored F3s carried a single pickup roller.

Prior to 1955, the sideframes for the Santa Fe, Western Pacific, and *Texas Special* were painted a very striking and elegant-looking silver. (The New York Central's were painted gray, and the Southern were painted black.) Although some early examples of the 2363 Illinois Central used sideframes that were painted black, from 1955 through 1966 sideframes for all F3s were chemically blackened.

Once again the horn began its annual migration. This time it was moved back into the power unit, but it was secured differently. For some reason, Lionel took a close look at the horn battery and its holding mechanisms in 1955. For starters, the lock screw that held the battery swivel-plate in place was smoother than in prior years. The plates used early in 1955 were identical to those used in prior years; however, during production they were replaced by new plates that were smooth and didn't contain etched information. This version was used without change through 1966.

Starting in 1955, workers on the assembly line began affixing stickers that described the operation of the horn and reminded customers to remove the D-cell battery from the locomotive before storing it. Some workers applied the sticker to the swivel-plate; others stuck them on the molded-in, L-shaped area on the underside of the fuel tank. The sticker actually seems to belong in the latter position, but it may have proved easier for assemblers to stick it to the swivel-plate. Perhaps the thinking was that the sticker would adhere to the smooth, shiny metal better than to the painted die-cast metal.

The portholes on the B unit, as well as those of the A, were filled in and became part of the casting (one way to solve the problem of lenses falling out). By removing the shell from the frame, you'll notice an impression of the porthole still present on the inside. The B unit's frame was also modified to accommodate the newly redesigned trucks and sideframes.

Variations: The first *Texas Specials* produced in 1955 still carried 1954 features: porthole windows with snap-in lenses and horizontal motors. The *Texas Special* was the only true carryover from 1954 and was produced using current methods. However, later models of the *Texas Special* were produced using 1955 specifications, creating one of the most desirable of all F3 variations.

Although the A-unit shell was still the same as produced in 1954, the frame was the same as the one used for the new 2243 Santa Fe. The truck sideframes were blackened instead of painted silver, the pilot was painted silver instead of red, and the motor was mounted vertically instead of horizontally.

The B-unit shell was a different matter. The portholes were filled in and became part of the casting. The frame was the same as that of the 2243 Santa Fe, which had the chemically blackened sideframes, unlike examples from 1954, which were painted silver.

Illinois Central 2363s can be found with rubber-stamped lettering in both brown and black. The brown-lettered version apparently came first and is harder to find. The brown- and black-letter variations are well known to collectors.

During the first production run of the Illinois Central, the pilot was painted black after assembly of the entire front top plate. This is evident from black paint overspray on the top plate and sideframes. At some point in the production cycle, the process was changed so that painting was done prior to assembly, evident from the absence of black overspray.

The A-unit shell for the 2363 Illinois Central was molded, as was the 2243 Santa Fe, in gray plastic and then painted and striped in the appropriate colors. Orange plastic was available for use in body shells and would seem to have been a natural choice for the Illinois Central; however, orange A-unit shells weren't used until 1957.

The B-unit shell for the Illinois Central, on the other hand, was molded in orange plastic (the Santa Fe B was gray) and then painted in the appropriate colors. Yellow stripes were rubber-stamped both above and below the orange band. The earliest B units had an unpainted orange band; on units produced later in the run, the band was painted orange.

The orange-plastic version is harder to find in good condition because the rubber-stamped lettering did not adhere well to the bare plastic. It's also worth noting that of the B units we've examined, these earliest examples have had brown rubber-stamped lettering only. It's not certain if any black rubber-stamped versions were actually made.

Two years' production of the 2245 *Texas Special.* In back is the 1954 version distinguished by its red pilot and portholes in both A and B units; in front is the 1955 version on a Santa Fe-type frame. The portholes on the B unit have been plugged.

1955 ORANGE-MOLDED F3A BODY SHELLS

By Frank Piazza

Sometime in 1955, Lionel produced orange plastic F3A body shells; Lionel also produced orange F3B shells that year. The B-unit shells were used for the 2363 Illinois Central, but no matching orange-shell Illinois Central A units are known to exist. Regular-production 2363 A units have gray plastic shells.

Orange shells show up fairly often on 2243 Santa Fe A units and somewhat less often on 2379 Rio Grande and 2373 Canadian Pacific A units.

Why did Lionel produce orange A-unit shells in 1955 if not to use them? And why weren't they used for the 2363 Illinois Central, as one might expect, given the orange-shell 2363 B units? Was it originally Lionel's intention to use the orange shells on Illinois Central A units, and then, for some reason, they used gray shells instead? Unfortunately, we probably won't know unless someone can resurrect historical Lionel production data and make it available.

There are two characteristics unique to 1955 A-unit tooling:

- Molded, raised cab-door ladders
- Deeper recess of the cab nose door handle.

The F3 tooling for 1955 represents Lionel's continued efforts at reducing production costs by eliminating labor-intensive assembly operations on F3 cabs. Detail was now cast into the body mold, and lower-cost details (for example, one-piece horns) were added as required. Shells produced for 1956 F3A units have different characteristics, since the changes are for reasons other than those described above.

Oddly, the 1955 orange-molded F3A shells, not used in 1955, went unused in 1956 as well. What was Lionel waiting for?

All the regular-production F3A units from 1957 have gray shells; however, 1955 orange-molded F3A shells show up frequently on 2243 Santa Fe A units and not so frequently on the 2379 Rio Grande A and the 2373 Canadian Pacific A.

Why did Lionel wait until 1957 to use up this inventory of 1955 orange-molded F3A shells? Was the inventory misplaced, did the vendor not deliver on time, or was there some other reason? By 1957, Lionel was no longer producing the 2363 Illinois Central, so the 1955 orange-molded F3A shells were used for locomotives that were in the line. Remember, Lionel's business was making toy trains, not manufacturing collectibles or variations.

A few years ago I purchased a 1958 no. 2383 Santa Fe in a master carton. The boxes looked just as they did the day Lionel packaged them. The dummy A unit was still factory sealed. The gentleman I bought the train from told me he had purchased the 2383 from a Blue Star Auto store and had test-run the powered A unit only to see if it worked.

I had little reason to doubt what he told me, because the powered unit was in perfect condition and showed no signs of wear. I came home satisfied that I had found a 1958 Santa Fe 2383 in perfect shape. I wanted it for my F3 collection, because 1958 was the first year the 2383 was cataloged.

Several years later, I got up enough nerve to break open the sealed dummy unit carton. I was surprised to find it had a 1955 orange-molded F3A shell, with the correct 2383 number boards, making it 1958 production!

Proof once again that Lionel used inventory as it best suited their needs. They were making toys, not collectibles.

Shown here are two 2363C Illinois Central B units (1955). The top one features an unpainted orange band and brown rubber-stamped lettering; the bottom unit has a painted orange band and black rubber-stamped lettering.

Wabash 2367 A and B units displayed the features introduced with 1955 production. Both the A and B shells were molded in royal blue plastic; however, the A unit was painted blue, while the B unit remained unpainted.

The 2367 Wabash had yellow heat-stamped lettering. Some early B units, however, had yellow rubber-stamped lettering and carried "Built by Lionel" on the same end of the cab, unlike the heat-stamped versions, which had "Built by Lionel" on the opposite ends. The rubber-stamped version is very hard to find and is another desirable F3 variation.

1956

Lionel once again carried two dual-motored F3s in their O gauge line, with the 2368 Baltimore & Ohio (an eastern road again) and 2378 Milwaukee Road (another midwestern) heading freight sets. The 2356 Southern, 2363 Illinois Central, and 2367 Wabash were still cataloged for separate sale but represented leftover inventory from the previous years. The single-motored 2240 Wabash AB joined the O-27 line, replacing the discontinued 2245 *Texas Special*.

Exterior features or trim (shell and trucks): Production of F3s in 1956 was, in terms of details, essentially the same as 1955. One recognizable change to the A-unit shell was that of recessing the molded cab ladders to make them flush with the cab sides, instead of raised. One explanation can be found in observing the paint on raised and flush models. Because the raised ones protrude beyond the sides of the shell – the ladders are the "high point" – paint tended to get rubbed off here first. Making the ladder flush kept the paint from getting chipped or rubbed off as readily. Perhaps more to the point, the flush ladders may have been needed to accommodate the new

A striking 2368 Baltimore & Ohio F3 AB consist from 1956.

The 2367 Wabash F3 AB from 1955 is in the foreground, while the 2240 single-motored AB from 1956 is shown in back.

heat-stamping and silk-screening processes used on the 2368 and 2378.

For every rule, of course, there is an exception. Uncataloged set no. 1535W, probably the last F3 set produced in 1955, is known to contain the flush-cab version of the 2243 Santa Fe, suggesting that the change was made before the end of the 1955 production year.

The change to a flush ladder undoubtedly saved time and money in another way as well. The flat side meant that the shell could be more easily masked for painting, striping, and lettering. This was true with regard to 1956 production of the 2240 Wabash and 2243 Santa Fe, and especially true for the 2368 Baltimore & Ohio and the 2378 Milwaukee Road.

In terms of saving money, the Milwaukee Road F3 was a good choice as an addition to the locomotive roster. Lionel simply molded the shell for the 2378 in the appropriate color of gray, thus leaving only the band and stripes to be applied.

For the Baltimore & Ohio, Lionel used a light blue plastic shell. They painted the roof gray and the top of the nose and sides white, and they left the blue unpainted, relying on the shell for the body color and saving on paint and set-up costs and application and drying time.

Lionel molded the 2240 Wabash shell in medium-blue (with a touch of purple) plastic (the 2367 Wabash shell was a royal blue) and

Uncataloged set 1535W, probably the last F3 set produced in 1955, contains the flush-cab 2243 Santa Fe.

The 2363 Illinois Central (left) from 1955 features a raised ladder; the 2379 Denver & Rio Grande Western (right) from 1957 features the flush ladder.

Set no. 810 (1956), featuring Milwaukee Road F3 AB units, has the distinction of being the first Lionel F3 set to include a major accessory, in this case, the no. 342 Culvert Loader.

Right: Note the full-length stripe on the 2367 (top) that stops short of the end of the Wabash 2240 B unit (bottom).

Far right: This production sample from Lionel's archives provides evidence that by 9/17/56 the white stripe on the Wabash B unit was short, as indicated on both the unit and the box.

Set no. 2269W (1956) featured the beautiful Baltimore & Ohio F3 AB.

then painted it in the appropriate blue, gray, and white. In the case of the 2240, unlike some of the other Fs, the entire body was painted; there were no production savings here.

Although the numbers for the 2240 and 2367 Wabash A units were stamped on the outside of the shells, the B units were not stamped and so are sometimes mismatched by collectors and operators. There are at least two ways to distinguish between them. One is to look on the inside of the body shell to identify the medium-blue plastic of the 2240 B unit (painted exterior, as with the A units), as compared to the royal blue (unpainted) of the 2367. Another clue can be found in the full-length white stripe of the 2367 B unit from 1955 as compared to the less-than-full-length white stripe of the 2240 B unit.

Finally, during 1956 production a plastic coupler-centering plunger for the front truck assembly replaced the metal plunger of 1955 and earlier. Note: The 1955 black-truck version of the 2245 *Texas Special* must have the metal coupler centering plunger.

Interior Features (frame assembly and shell): Starting with 1956 production, Lionel power frames were "spot faced" instead of wiped clean, which was a 1955 feature. The reason for both methods was to provide electrical grounding to the frame (silver metallic paint, as used in Santa Fe F3s and *Texas Specials,* is a conductor, whereas regular nonmetallic pigment is an insulator).

B-unit production was the same as 1955, except that during the molding of the gray and light blue plastic shells, a slight shadow or pressure point became noticeable above the inside door window nearest the roof vents.

Variations: The best-known variation of 1956 production is the 2378 Milwaukee Road with and without the yellow stripe along the roof line. The yellow-stripe version may have been an early experimental model that was discontinued once Lionel decided the extra striping was too time-consuming to produce. The yellow-stripe version is harder to find and a favorite with collectors.

In addition, some Milwaukee Road F3s were sold mismatched; i.e., an A unit without the yellow stripe coming with a B unit with the stripe. Overproduction of B units or damage to A units may account for the difference.

This 2378 Milwaukee Road AB from 1956 came as a mix-and-match pair. Note the yellow stripe along the top of the B unit and the absence of a stripe on the A unit.

The painting (or "unpainting") of shells has baffled collectors for years and has resulted in a number of reported variations. The two 1956 F-unit variations that are most difficult to find are a 2240 Wabash A-unit shell painted over the same light-blue plastic as the previously mentioned 2368 Baltimore & Ohio, and a 2368 A unit painted over a gray plastic shell. The gray 2368 version may have been a late 1956 or early 1957 replacement shell.

1957

Production for Lionel's 1957 roster is most notable (apart from Super O track and the pink Girl's Train, of course) for the return after 3 years of a deluxe passenger train pulled by a set of AA units: the Canadian Pacific set. The 2373 Canadian Pacific AA and 2379 Denver & Rio Grande Western AB, two new O gauge diesels, replaced the discontinued Baltimore & Ohio and Milwaukee Road units.

On the O-27 scene, the 2240 Wabash was dropped, and the 2243 Santa Fe was moved into the O gauge section of the catalog as the Alco locomotive series (in a "cheapened" version) was reintroduced.

Exterior Features or Trim (shell and trucks): Lionel made no significant changes from 1956 production, except for the occasional use of orange plastic shells for the 2243 Santa Fe, 2373 Canadian Pacific, and 2379 Denver & Rio Grande Western. Also, some 2378 dark-gray plastic cabs were decorated for the 2373 Canadian Pacific.

Interior Features (frame assembly and shell): Also the same as 1956, except that the E-unit was wired directly to the front motor, whereas in 1955 and 1956 it was wired to the rear motor. The battery opening on the dummy A was now filled in.

Shown here is a 2373 Canadian Pacific F3 AA set from 1957. The boxes in this set are among the most valuable of the Postwar period.

Set no. 2296W (1957) featured Canadian Pacific F3 AA units and marked the return of deluxe passenger sets. It was packed in a Super O-style box.

New in 1957 was the 2379 Denver & Rio Grande Western F3 AB in its handsome yellow-and-green scheme.

LIONEL F3 PRODUCTION HISTORY: 1958–1966

The only new paint scheme produced during the last years of Lionel's Postwar period was the 2242 New Haven from 1958 (right). The Santa Fe warbonnet was the only F3 paint scheme to be offered from start to finish.

1958

BASED SOLELY on the new paint schemes produced in 1957, you might expect that it had been a pretty good year for Lionel. The Canadian Pacific set was spectacular, and the bright yellow and green of the Denver & Rio Grande Western units looked striking. However, as Lionel prepared for Toy Fair (held in New York City every spring), they must have been greatly concerned about the results of 1957. For the first time during the 1950s, Lionel's annual

The 2242 New Haven F3 AB from 1958 is colorful and notable as the last new F3 paint scheme. What's really significant in this photo, however, is the master carton – perhaps the rarest of all Postwar F3 master cartons.

report to stockholders showed a net income of less than a million dollars ($842,076).

Later in 1958, Joshua Lionel Cowen, founder and driving force of the Lionel Corporation for nearly six decades, requested that he be relieved from the burden of day-to-day operational responsibilities. His request was honored, and he was offered – and accepted – the title of chairman emeritus of the board of directors.

Another change, though its potential long-range impact was probably not evident at the time, had to do with the public's changing perception of railroads. Passenger service was declining rapidly as equipment got older and railroads lost interest in customer service; freight service was also deteriorating as over-the-road trucks began to race coast-to-coast on the growing Interstate Highway System. Finally, airliners were now more glamorous, faster, and more efficient than the streamlined passenger trains pulled by F units! In short, the public was losing interest in trains – real ones and, unfortunately, Lionel toy trains (although it should be noted that HO scale model railroading was gaining in popularity).

During 1958 Lionel discontinued the 2243 Santa Fe, replacing it with the single-motored 2242 New Haven AB, which was cataloged heading a Super O freight set. The short-lived 2373 Canadian Pacific was also dropped from the line and was replaced by the reissue of the Santa Fe as a 2383 AA. The 2379 Denver & Rio Grande Western continued without change.

Exterior Features or Trim (shell and trucks): To accommodate the lettering of the New Haven, the front door handle was removed from the mold for the A-unit shell. In fact, the 1958 consumer catalog illustration shows the 2242 without the door handle. Remarkably, the same catalog shows the 2379 Rio Grande, which was produced first, with the door handle still in place, just as you'd expect. Now that's attention to detail! The illustration of the 2383 Santa Fe wasn't drawn with such detail; the door, much less the handle, doesn't even show.

Sometime during 1954 production of F3 A-unit shells, a small chip

The New Haven marks the end of the Postwar F3 era. The B units produced deserve coverage of their own (from left): New York Central, Santa Fe, *Texas Special*, Southern, Illinois Central, Wabash, Baltimore & Ohio, Milwaukee Road, Denver & Rio Grande Western, and New Haven.

The 1958 New Haven shell features a smooth door (note the handle on the New York Central). The change was apparently made to accommodate the NH herald.

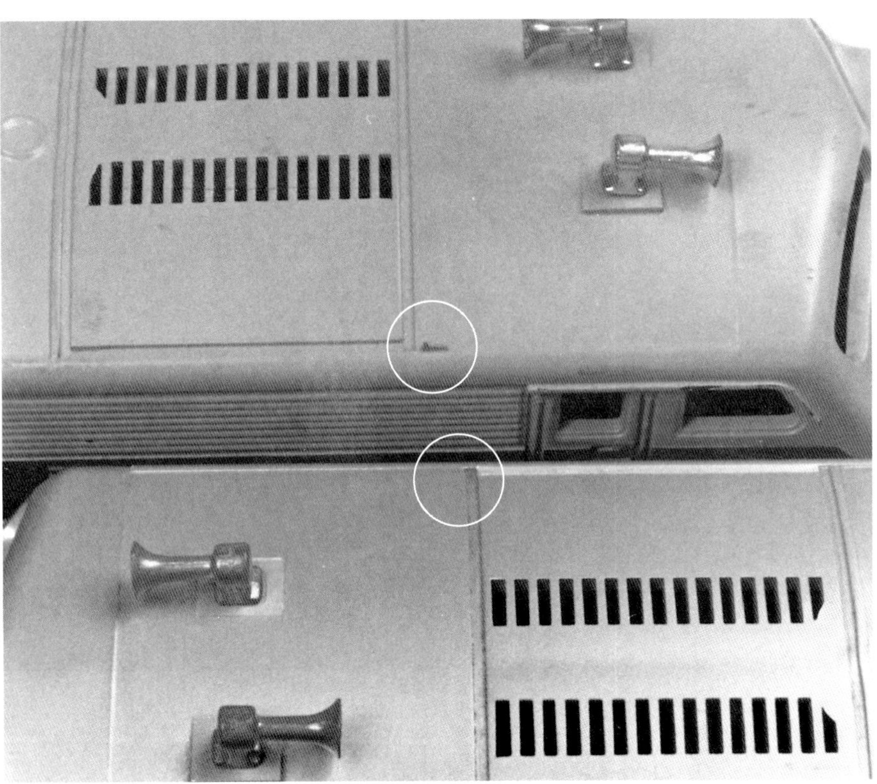

Note the tiny imperfection that began to show up in 1954 F3 models (in the roof just behind and above the locomotive door along the roofline). For some reason, in 1958 Lionel repaired the mold, and the "nubbin" (actually a nick out of the mold) is gone.

appeared in the tooling, resulting in an imperfection on the top of the cab. It's noticeable in all subsequently produced shells. In 1958, someone took the time to polish the tooling to eliminate the imperfection.

Another noticeable blemish was the dimple on the roof of the F3 cab. A sinkhole had developed, and the dimple began to sink forward into the plastic casting. This was recognizable on the 2383, which was probably the last F3 produced in 1958. Lionel would eventually eliminate the imperfection.

The rear truck for the 2242 New Haven used the dual-motor power truck casting without pickups. This was the only single-motored F3 to use this casting.

More disturbing, however, was the 1958 financial summary. Although net sales were at $14,463,825, the company experienced a net loss of $469,057. Though it didn't really matter where the loss came from, we toy train lovers can take satisfaction in knowing that 70 percent of the total consolidated loss was suffered by the Airex fishing tackle operation.

President Lawrence Cowen's year-end summary highlighted a certain confidence for 1959, though perhaps he was whistling in the dark for the stockholders' benefit, and an optimistic outlook for 1960. "The search for new items has been painstaking, and we believe that it is beginning to bear fruit. One such product, which we intend to carry into the test market stage soon, is an outboard motor. Our research

1959

As Lionel's fortunes spiraled downward, the F3 roster dwindled. In 1959 the 2379 Denver & Rio Grande Western was dropped from the line, leaving the New Haven and the Santa Fe as the only cataloged F3s.

The last version of the Postwar Santa Fe F3 (2383 AA from 1958) featured black sideframes and filled-in portholes. This was a stripped-down model compared to the classy units from 1948.

has indicated that we can hope to capture a reasonable part of the market. This is just one of several items under active consideration."

Needless to say, the idea never came to fruition. In hindsight, one wonders why Lionel would be considering outboard motors when the fishing tackle they already produced was losing so much money.

Exterior Features or Trim (shell and trucks): The Santa Fe depicted in the 1959 consumer catalog was done from the same base art as the 1958 illustration (undoubtedly a cost-saving measure). Both catalogs show the 2383 incorrectly with a red, instead of black, GM decal.

The nose decal for 1958, however, was correct, as the horizontal and vertical black lines appeared slightly broader than earlier examples. Sometime during 1959 production, the horizontal and vertical lines became thinner on some 2383 Santa Fe nose decals. This was probably just a matter of a different artist or decal supplier being used.

1960

Finally, the Santa Fe was forced to go it alone as the New Haven was dropped from the product line. For what it's worth, the consumer catalog (same base art again) still depicted the 2383 incorrectly with a red GM decal.

By the summer of 1960, Lionel's newest challenge, slot-car racing, was in full swing. Many hobby shops were tearing down Lionel train layouts and replacing them with slot-car tracks. The auto racing phenomenon turned out to be a relatively short-lived fad and didn't do much to hasten Lionel's downward slide. In retrospect, it was really more a case of adding insult to injury. In 1961 Lionel entered the slot-car market, but it was really a case of too little too late. At least management was trying.

1961

By 1961 the Santa Fe's red warbonnet appeared to have an orange tint to it. This color shift became more apparent in 1962 and 1963. Some Santa Fe units of the early 1950s have shown up with an orange cast to them, but this is probably due to fading. By removing the shell and inspecting the inside for paint overspray, you'll find that the color inside is red. By contrast, overspray inside Santa Fe shells from 1961 through 1963 has the same orange tint.

1962

If you look closely at the nose decals from this year's production, you'll note that the style and size of lettering changed. It very much resembles the lettering on the 2343 Santa Fe herald used during 1952 production. The letter "S" in Santa Fe now looks more like a backward "Z." (The backwards "Z" is prototypically correct. Note the "S" in the photo on page 7.) The 1962 consumer catalog illustrations clearly show the change. Perhaps Lionel switched vendors, or maybe a new artist modified the herald artwork sometime during 1961 or 1962 production. Or perhaps Lionel simply reused the decal artwork from 1952.

Dating back to 1948, F3 motors had copper windings coated with an insulating material. By 1962 the coating used for the armature windings had taken on a distinctly reddish tint. Also, by 1962 E-units were being wired to either the front or rear motors, apparently with no particular reason either way.

1963

The 1963 consumer catalog gives a pretty good indication of how things were going for Lionel. With the company unable or unwilling to pay for full-color printing, the catalog (except for the full-color cover) became a two-color book: black and red. With the color artwork went much of the magic it offered young and old model railroaders. Despite the economizing, there still was a fine assortment of trains from which to choose: ten O-27 and six Super O sets were cataloged.

The 2383 Santa Fe? It appears to have been simply a mixture of prior years' examples – whatever was still in the warehouse. It's as though Lionel was cleaning house, knowing that the end was near.

1964

The consumer catalog, this time in blue and black (including the cover), had perhaps the poorest selection – and illustration – of trains offered in the Postwar era. At this point Lionel was pursuing the manufacture and sale of uncataloged rather than cataloged sets.

The catalog illustration of the 2383 helps to distinguish the last external change to the Santa Fe. The black oval on the nose decal now fully surrounds the Santa Fe lettering, whereas in prior years the oval was interrupted by the horizontal lines of the herald. Also, the nose decals used in 1964 production feature noticeably thinner horizontal and vertical lines

1965

The consumer catalog was still pretty colorless (red, blue, and gold), but the trains were reasonably well displayed. The 2383 Santa Fe F3 that appeared in 1965 sets was a mixture of earlier examples, although the full-black-oval version didn't return until 1966. During 1965, the last noticeable interior change occurred: the motor-armature windings were green.

The decal nose herald continued to change (left to right): 1958, bold vertical and horizontal black stripes; 1964, thinner vertical and horizontal black stripes and a different S; 1966, medium-weight black stripes. Notice how the black line that defines the oval is broken at 3 o'clock and 9 o'clock on the first two heralds and that the oval on the right-hand locomotive is unbroken (not prototypically accurate).

1966

After three relatively colorless years, full color returned to the Lionel catalog, and the trains featured were photographs rather than artists' illustrations. Once again, the 2383 Santa Fe was a mixture of earlier examples, and the full-black-oval version was finally phased out. In fact, this last version of the 2383 was also a Lionel Service Station replacement shell. Many were wrapped and sent to Lionel dealers without the rear mounting bracket. The end was near.

Conclusion

For all practical purposes, the 2383 Santa Fe F3s produced from 1958 through 1966 were the same. The only notable differences had to do with nose decals, the roof dimple, the color of the red warbonnet, and the color of the armature windings. These are the primary clues that have been used to trace the sequence of F3 production.

In looking at the production history of Lionel's F3s, it's evident – and not surprising – that on occasion Lionel used or experimented with a variety of parts before deciding on the best one. In some cases parts may have been used interchangeably because it didn't matter; one was not clearly better than another. The odd or leftover parts were simply used until the supply was exhausted.

The fact that Lionel managers and employees changed and substituted parts and inventory as needed makes it possible that other apparent inconsistencies and variations will be found. Many questions will forever remain unanswered because, as far as we're aware, no one was keeping track of when the motor windings, for example, changed or why. All we can do is note that such changes happened, determine approximately when they happened, and speculate as to why.

Some interesting paint samples and a prototype. From the left, rear, is a Union Pacific F3 with a green nose; early Lionel FAs had a gray nose – the green is correct. In the center is a *Texas Special* with prototypically correct yellow stripes on the pilot. At right is a colorful, but never produced, Kansas City Southern unit. And the Pennsy unit in front is an odd double-cab locomotive that was never mass-produced.

This prototype is apparently a paint sample from 1958.

RICHARD KUGHN AND NICK DEGRAZIA, chief executives at Lionel Trains Inc., gave us permission to visit the Lionel archives and photograph appropriate F3 samples for this book. I would like to be able to report that the archives provided lots of answers to our questions. Unfortunately, that's not really the case. For starters, we couldn't rely on frames, shells, or trucks to help us determine production or development dates. Undoubtedly, the engineering department used whatever was available: leftover shells from previous years' production, frames from returned products, or trucks from current production. It is impossible at this point to tell.

The models, many of which are pictured here and on the following page, were interesting to look at and speculate about, but they didn't offer any conclusive evidence that might be of use in determining the F3's production history.

The majority of F3s in the archives are prototypes (usually denoted with the 0000 designation). The prototypes have a late-1950s flavor about them. For instance, the Alaska F3 was most likely contemplated during the same time the Alaska Set was brought out (in 1959), but that set was headed by a 614 Alaska switcher.

Most of the models were tagged but not dated. Those that were tagged with dates were regular production-line samples and were not really any help. For instance, the 2242C had a 9-24-58 date, but 1958 is a known year for its initial introduction to the product line. Verification, certainly, but not revelation. Some locomotives had two tags on them – a white one and another yellowed with age. The yellowed one seems to have come from the period the model was produced. The writing on the tags lists Section B and an XP (for "experimental"?) number.

One exception with regard to dated tags was the 2240C Wabash B unit. It had a Sept 17, 1956, date written on a piece of tape stretched across its roof. Although we already know that the 2240 AB was made only in 1956, the fact that the white interrupted stripe on the B unit didn't run the entire length of the shell was valuable information (the white interrupted stripe runs the entire length of a 2367C).

Another interesting find was a 2245 *Texas Special* with a "1954" tag. It had a 2355 number board (probably painted over a Western Pacific shell), and the front pilot was painted red with yellow stripes – just like the real thing. It's interesting to know that Lionel considered doing it right even though they probably discarded the idea as too time-consuming and expensive.

Another item of note is a green and yellow body shell with information written on the inside of the shell. The paint sample was described as XP 530, dated 1958, and with the following paint numbers: green 21-630 and yellow 11-902. Perhaps these were standard paint mix numbers so the colors could be duplicated should the sample be approved for addition to the regular line.

Without question, the most interesting "F3" in the archives is the double-cab Pennsylvania RR. The frame is actually two frames cut and spliced into one, and the Pennsy body is made up of two F-unit bodies. The resulting model is similar (though shorter) to Baldwin's DR-6-4-20, a double-cab locomotive owned by the Jersey Central. Another possibility is that this cobbled unit represents an early mock-up of what would become the double-cab EP-5. In fact, the tag on it refers to it as the "prototype electric engine."

So, while the archives, in this case, failed to produce any startling revelations, the paint schemes preserved there at least give us some insight into what Lionel's development engineers were thinking with regard to F3s.

An Alaska RR F3 that was never mass-produced, though an Alaska set was released in 1959.

This Atlantic Coast Line unit in its basic black paint scheme was never produced.

The Texas & Pacific, in blue, gray, and yellow, would have made a handsome F unit had it been mass-produced.

A Minneapolis & St. Louis paint sample. M&StL Geep (no. 2348) was produced in 1958, and the 6464-525 boxcar lettered for the M&StL was offered in 1957. Some connection seems likely.

ECONOMY F3

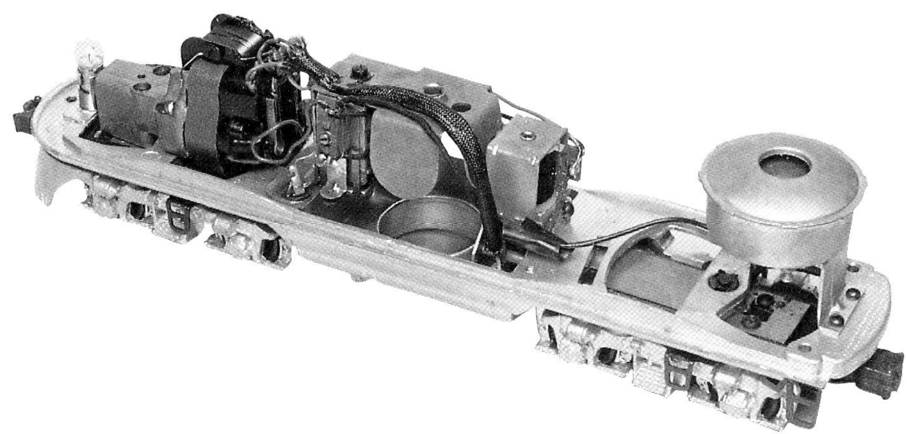

While doing research for this book in the Kalmbach Publishing Co. library, I came across an ad in the November 1950 issue of *Model Railroader.* The ad touted an "Economy Unit Lionel Diesel" and described it as having "one motor, one unit, less horn, Santa Fe or NYC with Magne-Traction." The advertiser was Fischer's Hobby Service of Louisville, Kentucky. The description of this single-motored unit from 1950 started ringing some bells concerning a puzzling locomotive I had bought a few years earlier. As I paged through more issues of MR, I came across Fischer's Hobby Service again, this time in the Trade Topics column. Apparently they were converting Lionel hoppers to hoppers for use on scale model railroads by adding scale trucks. Accomplished kitbasher, this Fischer!

When I got back home, I pulled out the locomotive I was thinking of and examined it. I remembered it being part of a purchase that included two train sets — the real objects of my interest. The single Santa Fe F3 from 1950 had still been in its box stamped 2343P; I recall pulling the A unit out of the box and thinking how light it seemed. When I removed its shell, I was surprised to find a power truck on front, but a horn mounted over the rear, unpowered truck. The horn mounting was neat, but obviously not done at the factory. My conclusion at the time was that someone had tampered with it, though I couldn't imagine why they would convert this to a single-motored unit.

I don't know for sure that this is a Fischer product, but the clues seem to point in that direction. If it is, then somewhere out in the land of Lionel collectors or operators there ought to be at least one 2343T (trailer) with a single motor and horn.

Lionel Hopper Cars Converted by Fischer

given this preparation and treatment with the same results.

Rivet detail on the oxidized and painted loco was rubbed with the fingers to simulate handling. After several minutes of this, the paint still had not worn off.

We definitely like this primer — on the metals for which it was intended — as a preparation for a durable paint job.

The company states that Roundhouse paint is not paint or lacquer in the gen-

per 48 cc. jar. Thinner comes in 2, 8 and 16-ounce sizes at 25, 45 and 75 cents, respectively. A descriptive and instructive painting guide is available free.

O Gauge Tinplate Freight Cars

Fischer's Hobby Service

618 S. Fourth St., Louisville, Ky.

Price: See below

Tinplaters who like variety in their roll-

ECONOMY UNIT

LIONEL DIESEL

$23.50

One motor, one unit, less horn

Santa Fe or NYC with Magne-Traction

REGULAR LIONEL DIESEL

Santa Fe or NYC **$42.50**

Complete Stock in all Gauges

Scale & Tinplate

All prepaid orders sent postpaid

FISCHER'S HOBBY SERVICE

618 S. FOURTH STREET

LOUISVILLE, KY.

Repaints and Reproductions

Ed Kraemer was one of the early repaint artists in the hobby. These are samples of his work, probably painted on Fundimensions shells.

Kraemer reproductions can be identified because he stamped his name on the inside of the shells.

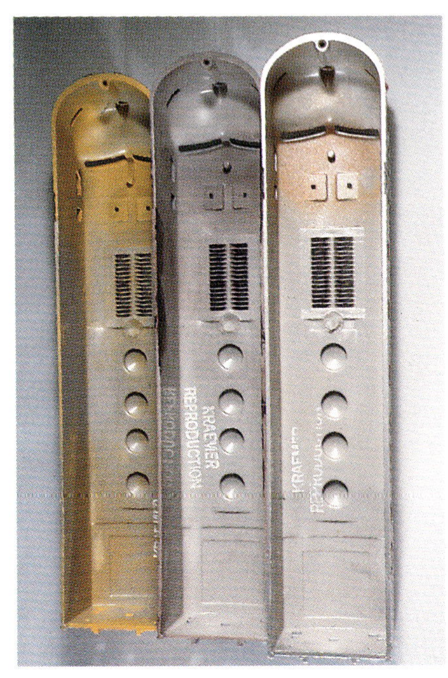

DURING THE LATE 1960s and early 1970s, Lionel Postwar F3s were reported by hobbyshop owners everywhere as being rare (train meets didn't really become popular until the mid-1970s, and before that, hobbyshop owners were the primary buyers and sellers of trains). Of course, Lionel's purchase by General Mills in 1969 added to the concern that F3 production would come to an end, making F3s truly "rare."

This concern resulted in at least three responses:

- The price of original Lionel equipment, especially F3s, began to increase
- Many collectors, convinced of the rarity of F3s and believing they would never be able to own an original, settled for a reasonable – though repainted – facsimile
- Operators were convinced not to run an original for fear of decreasing the F3's collectible value.

These factors, in turn, resulted in a new market of repainted and

Lionel B units were also subject to repainting. Many repainters worked on shells in poor condition – but not all of them were so selective.

restored trains. Some repainters were simply trying to satisfy the legitimate concerns of collectors (who thought they'd never own a Western Pacific, for instance) and operators (who believed it was okay to run a repainted engine). Others saw a handsome buck to be made and took advantage of the market demand, knowingly putting repaints on the market and offering them as originals.

Not all locomotives were in collectible shape or, for that matter, even "repaintable" shape. Parts were missing or broken and could be put back into the market only after the engine was put back into running shape. At first, this meant swapping parts from other "junkers" to make one complete unit. Eventually, though, reproduction parts began to show up.

Thus, repaints and reproduction parts have led to the confused market that exists today. The accompanying decoration and reproduction charts should help clear up some of that confusion.

ORIGINAL LIONEL F3s VS. REPRODUCTIONS

Lettering

No.	Road Name	Shell Color	Lettering (Original)	Lettering (Reproduction)
2240	Wabash	Med. Blue	Heat-stamped	Silk-screened
2242	New Haven	Gray	Heat-stamped	Silk-screened
2243	Santa Fe	Gray	Heat-stamped	Silk-screened
2245	*Texas Special*	Gray	Reversed-out	Silk-screened
2333	Santa Fe (1948)	Black	Rubber-stamped	Silk-screened
2333	NYC (1948)	Black	Rubber-stamped	Silk-screened
2333	Santa Fe (1949)	Black	Heat-stamped	Silk-screened
2333	NYC (1949)	Black	Heat-stamped	Silk-screened
2343	Santa Fe	Bk,Y, Gr	Heat-stamped	Silk-screened
2344	NYC	Bk,Y, Gr	Heat-stamped	Silk-screened
2345	Western Pacific	Gray	Heat-stamped	Silk-screened
2353	Santa Fe	Gray	Heat-stamped	Silk-screened
2354	NYC	Gray	Heat-stamped	Silk-screened
2355	Western Pacific	Gray	Heat-stamped	Silk-screened
2356	Southern	Gray	Rubber-stamped	Silk-screened
2363	Illinois Central	Gray	Rubber-stamped	Silk-screened
2367	Wabash	Royal Blue	Heat-stamped	Silk-screened
2368	B & O	Light Blue	Heat-stamped	Silk-screened
2373	Canadian Pacific	Gray	Heat-stamped	Silk-screened
2378	Milwaukee Road	Dark Gray	Heat-stamped	Silk-screened
2379	Rio Grande	Gray	Heat-stamped	Silk-screened
2383	Santa Fe	Gray	Heat-stamped	Silk-screened

Note: Variations are explained in greater detail in text.

Nose Herald

No.	Road Name	Nose Herald (Original)	Nose Herald (Reproduction)
2240	Wabash	Decal	Decal
2242	New Haven	Heat-stamped	Decal/Silk-screened
2243	Santa Fe	Decal	Decal
2245	*Texas Special*	Silk-screened	Silk-screened
2333	Santa Fe	Decal	Decal
2333	NYC	Decal	Decal
2343	Santa Fe	Decal	Decal
2344	NYC	Decal	Decal
2345	Western Pacific	Decal	Decal
2353	Santa Fe	Decal	Decal
2354	NYC	Decal	Decal
2355	Western Pacific	Decal	Decal
2356	Southern	Decal	Decal
2363	Illinois Central	Decal	Decal
2367	Wabash	Decal	Decal
2368	B&O	Rubber-stamped	Decal/Silk-screened
2379	Rio Grande	Decal	Decal
2383	Santa Fe	Decal	Decal

The text provides additional information on variations that were caused by chance (color of plastic shell), or rubber-stamped versus heat-stamped.

Lionel's silk-screening process was coarser than modern reproductions. The main difference, however, is that original lettering was not silk-screened.

Side Stripes and/or Band

No.	Road Name	Side Stripes (Original)	Side Stripes (Reproduction)
2240	Wabash	Silk-screened	Silk-screened
2242	New Haven	Not applicable	Not applicable
2243	Santa Fe	Rubber-stamped	Silk-screened
2245	*Texas Special*	Silk-screened	Silk-screened
2333	Santa Fe	Rubber-stamped	Silk-screened
2333	NYC	Rubber-stamped	Silk-screened
2343	Santa Fe	Rubber-stamped	Silk-screened
2344	NYC	Rubber-stamped	Silk-screened
2345	Western Pacific	Not applicable	Not applicable
2353	Santa Fe	Rubber-stamped	Silk-screened
2354	NYC	Rubber-stamped	Silk-screened
2355	Western Pacific	Not applicable	Not applicable
2356	Southern	Rubber-stamped	Silk-screened
2363	Illinois Central	Rubber-stamped	Silk-screened
2367	Wabash	Silk-screened	Silk-screened
2368	B & O	Rubber-stamped	Silk-screened
2373	Canadian Pacific	H/S stripes	Silk-screened
2378	Milwaukee Road	Silk-screened, H/S lines	Silk-screened
2379	Rio Grande	Silk-screened, H/S lines	Silk-screened
2383	Santa Fe	Rubber-stamped	Silk-screened

REPRODUCTION F3 PARTS

The following is a partial list of reproduction/replacement parts known to be available as this book went to press. Undoubtedly, others are – or will become – available. For more information, consult your nearest Lionel Service Station or parts dealer. Check ads in *Classic Toy Trains* magazine for parts dealers as well.

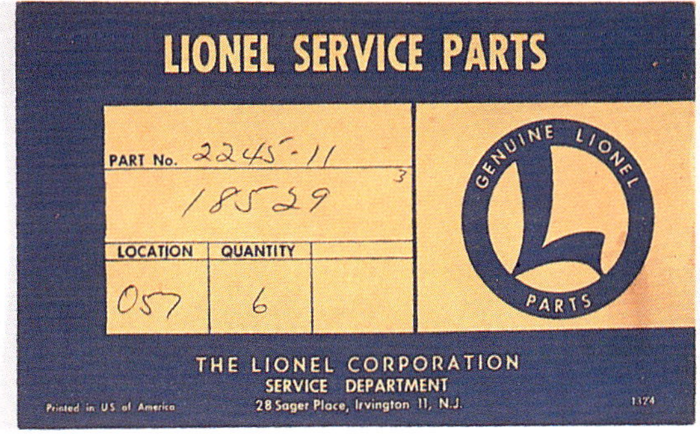
LIONEL SERVICE PARTS

PART No. 2245-11
18529

LOCATION	QUANTITY
057	6

GENUINE LIONEL PARTS

THE LIONEL CORPORATION
SERVICE DEPARTMENT
28 Sager Place, Irvington 11, N.J.

Printed in U.S. of America

Original decals (these were for the *Texas Special*) were available for purchase by hobbyists well into the 1970s.

Part Number	Description
2-111	Lock Washer
6TC-10	Coil Coupler Head
6TC-12	Collector Shoe Spring
45-73	Lock Washer
61-22	Lamp Contact
100-5	Reversing Unit
167-20	Speed Nut
480-18	Retaining Washer
480-20	Collector Shoe Rivet
622-138	Collector Roller
622-145	Collector Spring RH
622-146	Collector Spring LH
671-21	Axle (Knurled)
1447-300	Lamp (18-volt/ Bayonet Type)
2020M-33	Motor Brush
2020M-34	Brush Spring
2023-44	Roller Pin
2245-11	Decal RH (*Texas Special*)
2245-12	Decal LH (*Texas Special*)
2332-7	Ornamental Horn
*2333-6	Marker Lens RH
*2333-10	Marker Lens LH
2333-12	Wire Ventilator (Screen)
2333-13	Twin Speed Nut (Ventilator)
2333-14	Side Windows (Porthole Lens)
2333-15	Door Ladder (Cab)
2333-16	Grab Handle
2333-23	Rear Ladder (Frame)
2333-25	Window Shell
2333-26	Nose Decal (Santa Fe)
2333-42	Insulating Washer (Collector)
2333-53	Pivot Stud (Truck)
2333-57	Ladder RH
2333-587	Ladder LH
2333-60	Coupler and Drawbar Assembly
2333-62	Shield (Front Coupler)
2333-63	Shield Screw
2333-64	Drawbar Centering Spring
2333-65	Worm Shaft Bearing Assembly
2333-74	Coupler Retaining Plate
2333-75	Dummy Coupler (Rear Truck)
2333-104	Decal (GM)
2333-115	Shoulder Rivet
2333-116	Lock Screw
2333-128	Rubber Grommet
2333-130	Worm Wheel
2333M-14	Drive Gear
2333-4	Decal (GM)
2334-23	Nose Decal (NYC)
2343-33	Drive Wheel
2343-37	Worm Wheel
2343-55	Horn
2343-69	Decal B Unit (Santa Fe)
2343-122	Nut Slotted (Brush Plate)
2345-11	Decal (Western Pacific)
2353-11	Side Window (Porthole Lens)
2356-11	Decal (Southern)
2363-15	Decal (Illinois Central)
2367-12	Decal (Wabash)
2373-10	Decal (Canadian Pacific)
2378-15	Decal (Milwaukee Road)
2379-10	Decal (Rio Grande)
R-91	Lamp Spring
TC-21	Coupler Knuckle
TC-22	Knuckle Spring
TC-23	Knuckle Rivet
TC-109	Collector Shoe Plate
TC-112	Plunger Spring
TC-113	Plunger (Coupler)
TT-208	Collector Shoe

***Note:** RH and LH marker lenses were reproduced for each F3 cataloged by Lionel.

"RARE" RUBBER-STAMPED 2333s

"Rare" rubber-stamped 2333 Santa Fe and New York Central F3s from 1949.

During the 1970s, the early rubber-stamped F3s were the first choice of custom-painters who needed shells for repainting. Why were these engines preferred? For starters, after 20 and more years of wear, the paint and rubber-stamped lettering had not held up all that well, and custom-painters were more likely to paint "beaters" than mint or excellent examples. From a purely economic point of view, they knew they could get more for their repaints than they could for an original in less-than-desirable condition.

Also, because rubber-stamped F3s tended to show their age, they were usually the least expensive to purchase, an important business consideration for the entrepreneurial custom-painter.

But perhaps even more important, custom-painters knew that the rubber-stamped shells were the best medium for their work. Unlike heat-stamped lettering, which is literally indented in the plastic, rubber-stamped lettering simply rests on the surface and is easy to remove. Once the rubber-stamped shells have been stripped, there's no indentation to mar the repaint.

Thus, early rubber-stamped 2333 New York Central and Santa Fe F3s, abundant during the late 1960s and early 1970s, became "rare." Those rubber-stamped 2333s that have survived in collections are not always in excellent to like-new condition, and upgrading is very difficult.

Repair and Maintenance

Tips for the Operator of the Lionel F3
By Joseph M. Bak Jr.

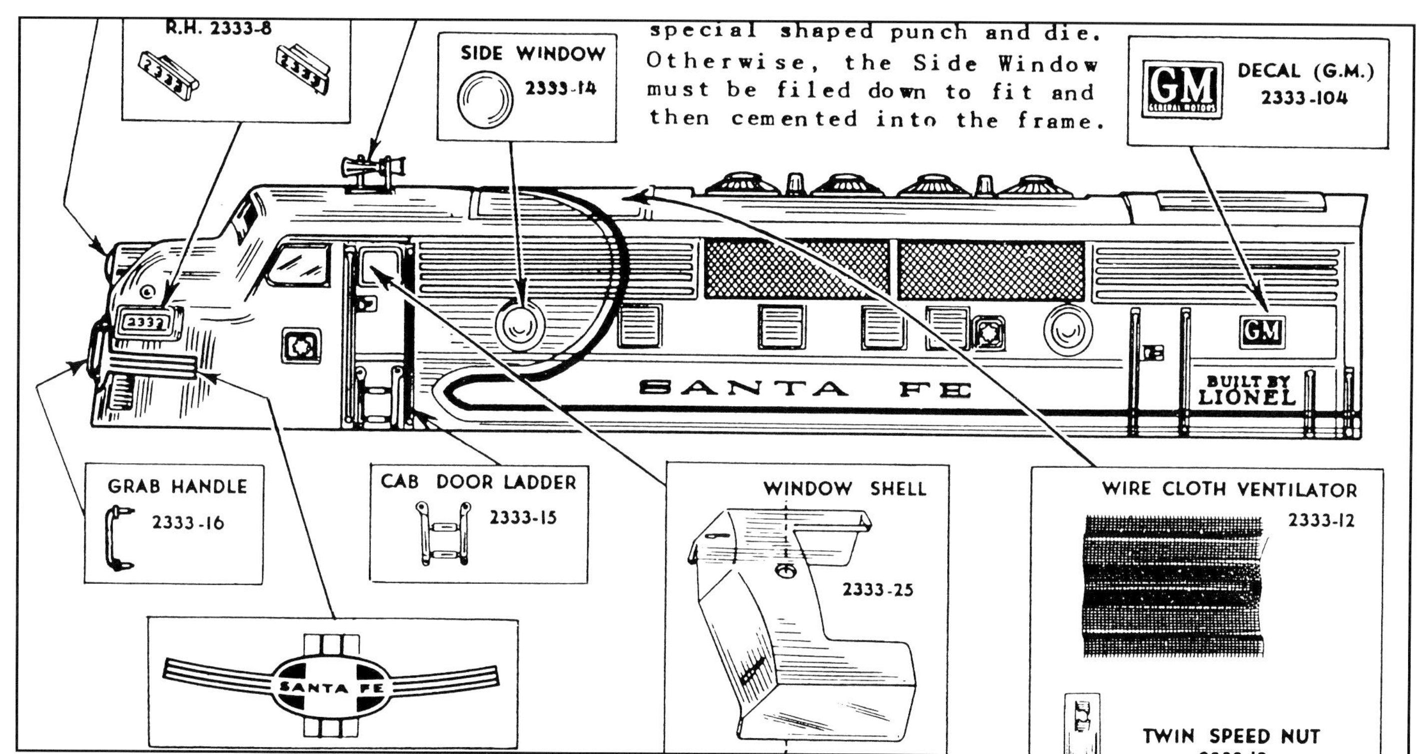

THE F3 WAS – and still is – a very reliable model and a fine runner. However, nothing was made to run forever, and the locomotive does require occasional lubrication and maintenance. If you follow the directions given in *Greenberg's Lionel Postwar Operating Instructions with Layout Plans,* the F3 should give you hours of entertainment and performance. Occasionally, however, mechanical and electrical devices fail. When that happens, you'll want to refer to your copy of *Greenberg's Repair and Operating Manual for Lionel Trains, 1945–1969.* This includes exploded-view diagrams of the single- and dual-motored versions, including part numbers, wiring schematics, and brief descriptions of some of the key changes to the locomotives.

Assuming that you have that reference material available and some mechanical and electrical aptitude, I will offer tips on repairing some of the Lionel F3's most common – or toughest – problems, both mechanical and electrical, that I've observed over several years of repairing Lionel trains.

During the Postwar era, Lionel produced three different F3 chassis or frame styles for use with all the road names they offered. Specific changes were introduced from year to year, and the author of this book has covered those in detail. I'll describe the basic repair principles, and you should be able to adapt them to the specific unit on which you're working. In describing the three versions, I usually refer to the representative Santa Fe models because so many people own this locomotive and because it was cataloged longer than any other F3.

The three chassis styles are represented by the 2333, 2343/53, and 2383 dual-motored units. The single-motored units are nearly identical to the 2383-type chassis. This single-motored version was also used for a while in the 1970s, during the Model Products Corp. (MPC) era. The later dual-motored MPC units follow the 2383 style; the 2343/53-type chassis was brought back by Lionel Trains Inc. (LTI). I won't touch on the problems of the F3s from those periods, though some of what follows will apply to the later models.

Wheels and Magnetic Axles

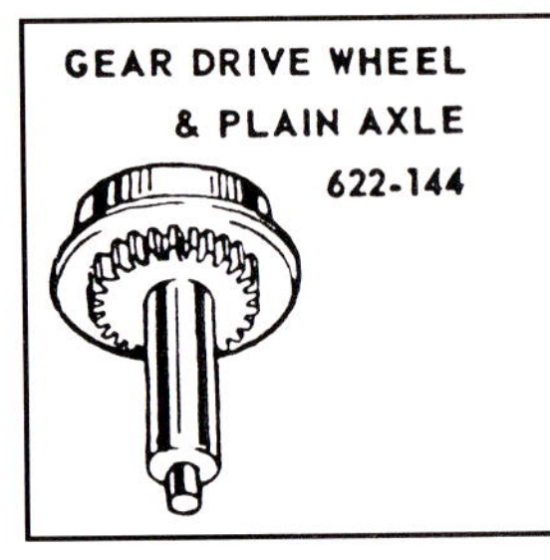

A problem can occur with the original Lionel powdered-iron wheels and magnetic axles used on the 2343/53 and 2383 chassis. The steel used for the ends of the magnetic axle can actually enlarge the hole in the powdered-iron wheel to the point that it will eventually spin freely and even begin to wobble. This wheel (part no. 2343-33) can easily be replaced from many sources.

The axle end itself can also become loose from the stainless steel tube it is encased in (along with the core of Alnico magnetic material) when the glue and rolled edges become weakened because of the torque of running for a long time. Sometimes, after removing the wheel and cleaning the area with denatured alcohol, you can flood the axle end with CA (cyanoacrylate adhesive, or "super glue") and stake the stainless-steel tubing with a chisel just enough to hold it in place.

For a more permanent repair, drill a small hole through the end of the axle and stainless-steel tubing at about a 15-degree angle. Insert a piece of piano wire into the hole and secure it with epoxy, trimming it to fit.

If neither of these approaches works, you'll need to buy a replacement part. This process can become confusing, since the axle is usually sold with a wheel mounted on it, and over the years Lionel listed in their manuals several wheel-and-axle assemblies designed for a variety of applications.

For example, magnetic axles that were designed to pass through a worm gear were different from those that did not (those passing through a worm wheel were swedged [or knurled], and those not

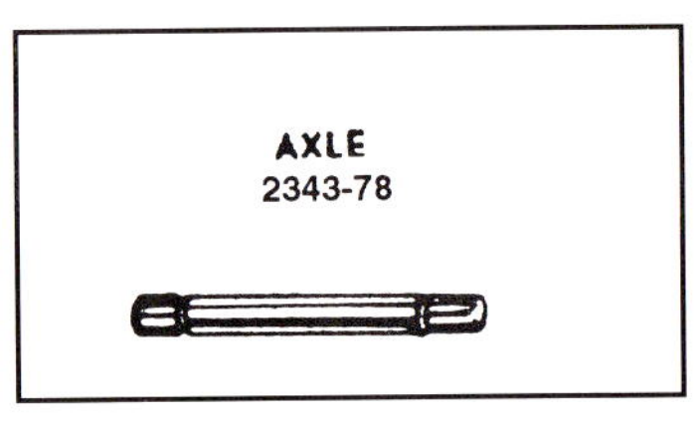

passing through a worm wheel were nonswedged [non-knurled]).

The part number for the magnetic axle is 2343-78 (replaced by 2353-29 for the swedged and 2353-30 for the non-swedged) but they have been shown as part number 622-143, 623-10, 623-13, or 2328-75 for the swedged magnetic axle assembly, and 622-144, or 2343-70 for the nonswedged axle assembly.

Brittle Wire

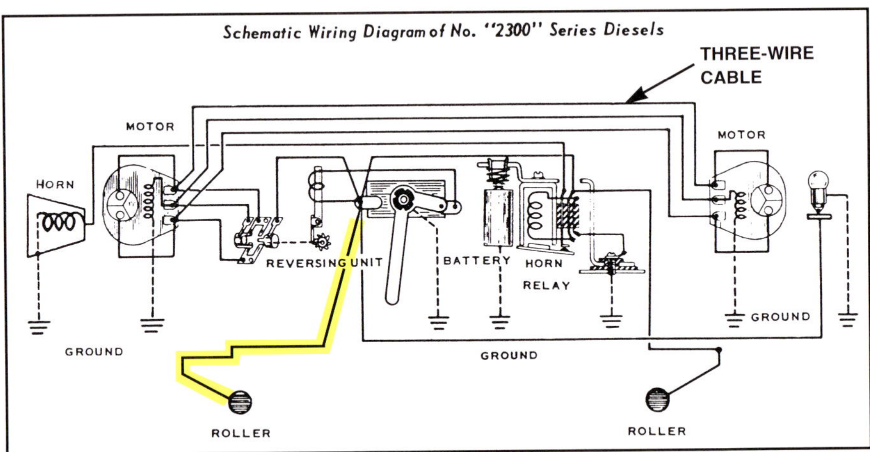

Another operational concern is the wire leading from the collector assembly to the lug on the reversing unit. Over the years, the rubber-coated wire of Lionel Postwar units has become stiff and brittle. Replace the lead from the collector assembly to the reversing-unit terminal lug, and from there to the first motor, with stranded PVC wire.

If the stranded three-wire cable between the motors looks tired, replace it as well. Shrink tubing, purchased at electronics supply stores, will cover the three leads nicely, insulate them completely, and cut down on the clutter inside the shell.

Motor Frame Rivet

The rivet that holds the field coil to the motor casting frame often comes loose, most likely due to vibration, electrolysis, or even poor riveting during manufacturing. This problem is mentioned in the manual for the 2333 back in 1949. "Occasionally, poor operation of the

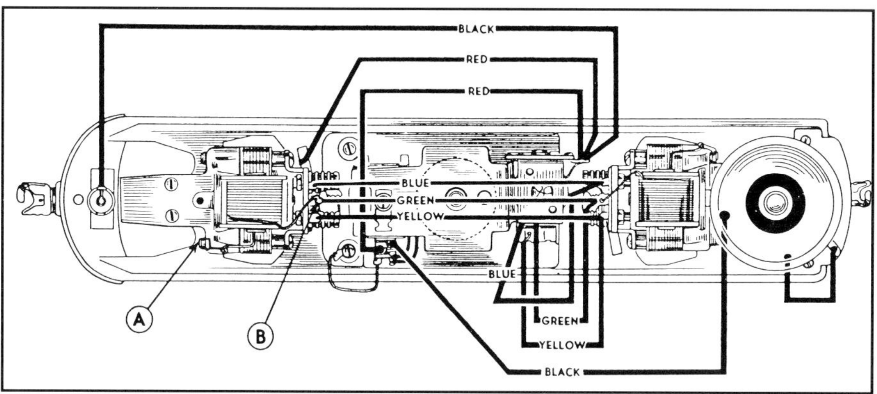

motor may be due to mechanical interference between the field and the armature caused by loose riveting of the field laminations." The problem can usually be corrected by tapping the star-shaped area of the rivet (point A on the accompanying diagrams) with the round end of a ball peen hammer or a large flat-head 12d (or larger) nail.

Do this with the brushplate removed and the field coil resting on the jaws of a vise. Make sure the threaded part of the rivet is firmly held by the vise jaws, otherwise you may push the rivet out from the field coils, loosening the laminations and eventually contributing to a noisy motor.

I usually heat the area of the restaked or flattened part of this rivet to relax the effect of cold-working the metal. This prevents it from cracking later; I sometimes even add solder to the area (acid flux with plain solder and thoroughly cleaned to prevent the corrosive effects of acid flux).

Commutator Face

Over time, carbon brush deposits tend to build up in the commutator slots and short two or more segments of the armature together.

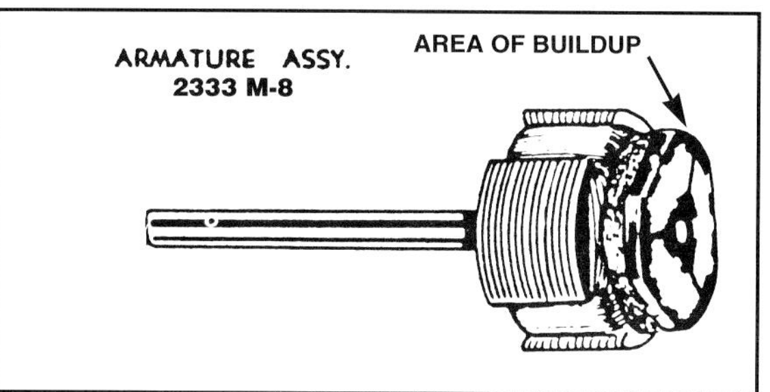

This carbon greatly slows down the motor and causes considerable heating that can lead to the motor's burning out. You'll notice this phenomenon when one power truck is running slower than the other; another indication is a "halo of fire" visible through the hole between the brushes on the motor brushplate.

A trick I use is to fill the slots of the commutator face with five-minute epoxy. Make sure you reface (smooth) the commutator face after the epoxy sets, otherwise the brushes will bounce, resulting in poor contact and eventually causing the brushes to chip and wear out sooner than normal.

Lubrication

Lubrication is critical for proper operation of the locomotive; however, for lubrication to be effective, it's important that you remove the grease, grime, and grit that have accumulated since the mechanism was last cleaned – especially if it has been several years since the locomotive has been operated.

The long-term evaporation of the lubricant can actually leave a varnish-like coating on the surface, and you might just as well try lubricating a painted part. Also, many of the currently available lubricants are synthetics and incompatible with the some of the materials and old lubrication, actually accelerating this problem.

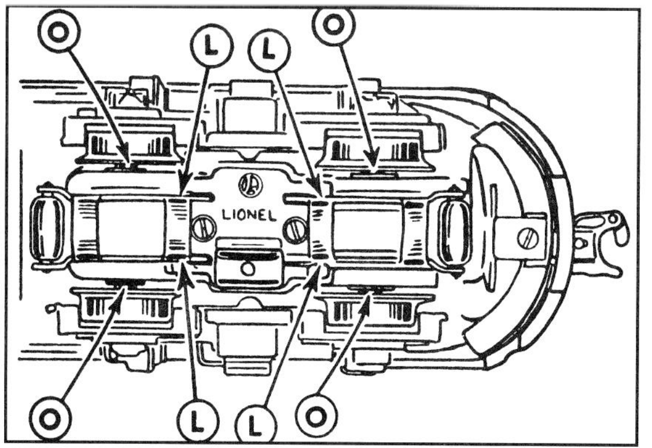

I have found that good old mineral spirits is the best solvent for soaking most of the old lubricants away. ***Do not use lacquer thinner, as it will dissolve the varnish coating off the wires of the armature and field coil.*** And I do

This (formerly mint-in-box) F3 was damaged by leakage from the factory-packaged battery. The owner was unaware of what was happening until he noticed the box damage.

mean soak – I leave the power trucks and motors in it for a couple of hours, if necessary, before hitting it with a toothbrush. ***Be sure to work with solvents only in a well-ventilated area and away from open flames. Also, protect your eyes and skin while working with solvents.***

I then flush the solvent off with a spray of hot, soapy water – briefly – and blow-dry the parts with a hair dryer.

When the mechanisms are thoroughly clean, I apply LaBelle no. 108 oil and no. 106 grease to the locations specified in the service manuals. Lots of greases and oils will work; the key is to make sure whatever brand you choose is safe for use with plastics. The label or packaging will let you know. Also, apply lubrication sparingly. Excess lubricant will eventually spray over the inside of the locomotive shell and work its way down to the wheels and track.

Horn

Perhaps the worst thing you can do is leave a dry-cell (size D) battery inside the locomotive. This may be the most common problem we find with F3s – damage caused by a leaky battery. It makes a mess.

Always remove those batteries, especially if the unit is going to sit around for a few months. There is no such thing as a really leak-proof battery. And once the damage is done, there's little you can do to repair the mechanism. Replacement becomes the only option.

APPENDIX A: CATALOGED SETS

1948	**2133W**	**$65.00**
	2333P/T	Santa Fe or New York Central F3s, AA
	2458	Automobile Car
	3459	Operating Ore Dump Car
	2555	Sunoco Oil Car
	2357	Lionel Caboose
1949	**2151W**	**$67.50**
	2333P/T	Santa Fe or New York Central F3s, AA
	3464	Operating Boxcar
	6555	Sunoco Oil Car
	3469	Operating Ore Dump Car
	6520	Operating Searchlight Car
	6457	Lionel Caboose
1950	**2161W**	**$67.50**
	2343P/T	Santa Fe Twin Diesel F3s, AA
	3469X	Operating Ore Dump Car
	3464	Operating Boxcar
	3461X	Operating Log Car
	6520	Operating Searchlight Car
	6457	Lionel Caboose
1950	**2171W**	**$67.50**
	2344P/T	New York Central Twin Diesel F3s, AA
	3469X	Operating Ore Dump Car
	3464	Operating Boxcar
	3461X	Operating Log Car
	6520	Operating Searchlight Car
	6457	Lionel Caboose
1950, 51	**2175W**	**$57.50, $70.00**
	2343P/T	Santa Fe Twin Diesel F3s, AA
	6456	Lehigh Valley Hopper, black, 50
	6456-50	Lehigh Valley Hopper, maroon, 51
	3464	Operating Boxcar
	6555	Sunoco Oil Car, 50
	6465	Sunoco Oil Car, 51
	6462	NYC Gondola Car
	6457	Lionel Caboose
1950, 51	**2185W**	**$57.50, $70.00**
	2344P/T	New York Central Twin Diesel F3s, AA
	6456	Lehigh Valley Hopper, black, 50
	6456-50	Lehigh Valley Hopper, maroon, 51
	3464	Operating Boxcar
	6555	Sunoco Oil Car, 50
	6465	Sunoco Oil Car, 51
	6462	NYC Gondola Car
	6457	Lionel Caboose
1952, 53	**2190W**	**$89.50**
	2343P/T	Santa Fe Twin Diesel F3s, AA, 52
	2353P/T	Santa Fe Twin Diesel F3s, AA, 53
	2533	Silver Cloud Pullman
	2532	Silver Range Vista Dome
	2534	Silver Bluff Pullman
	2531	Silver Dawn Observation
1952	**2191W**	**$70.00**
	2343P/T	Santa Fe Twin Diesel F3s, AA
	2343C	Santa Fe B Unit
	6462	NYC Gondola Car
	6656	Stock Car
	6456	Lehigh Valley Hopper
	6457	Lionel Caboose
1952	**2193W**	**$70.00**
	2344P/T	New York Central Twin Diesel F3s, AA
	2344C	New York Central B Unit
	6462	NYC Gondola Car
	6656	Stock Car
	6456	Lehigh Valley Hopper
	6457	Lionel Caboose
1953	**2207W**	**$70.00**
	2353P/T	Santa Fe Twin Diesel F3s, AA
	2343C	Santa Fe B Unit
	3484	Pennsylvania Operating Boxcar
	6415	Sunoco Oil Car
	6462	NYC Gondola Car
	6417	Pennsylvania Caboose
1953	**2209W**	**$70.00**
	2354P/T	New York Central Twin Diesel F3s, AA
	2344C	New York Central B Unit
	3484	Pennsylvania Operating Boxcar
	6415	Sunoco Oil Car
	6462	NYC Gondola Car
	6417	Pennsylvania Caboose
1954	**1517W**	**$59.95**
	2245P/C	The *Texas Special* F3, AB
	6464-225	Southern Pacific Boxcar
	6561	Lionel Lines Cable Car
	6462-25	NYC Gondola Car, green
	6427	Lionel Lines Caboose
1954	**1520W**	**$69.50**
	2245P/C	The *Texas Special* F3, AB
	2432	Clifton Vista-Dome
	2435	Elizabeth Pullman
	2436	Summit Observation
1954	**2227W**	**$69.50**
	2353P/T	Santa Fe Twin Diesel F3s, AA
	3562-25	Operating Barrel Car, gray
	6356	NYC Stock Car
	6456-75	Lehigh Valley Hopper, red
	6468	Automobile Car, blue
	6417-25	Lionel Lines Caboose
1954	**2229W**	**$69.50**
	2354P/T	New York Central Twin Diesel F3s, AA
	3562	Operating Barrel Car, gray
	6356	NYC Stock Car
	6456-75	Lehigh Valley Hopper, red
	6468	Automobile Car, blue
	6417-25	Lionel Lines Caboose
1954	**2231W**	**$79.50**
	2356P/T	Southern Twin Diesel F3s, AA
	2356C	Southern B Unit
	6561	Lionel Lines Cable Car
	6511	Lionel Pipe Car
	3482	Operating Milk Car with Platform
	6415	Sunoco Oil Car
	6417	Lionel Lines Caboose
1954	**2234W**	**$89.50**
	2353P/T	Santa Fe Twin Diesel F3s, AA
	2530	REA Baggage Car, small door
	2532	Silver Range Vista-Dome
	2533	Silver Cloud Pullman
	2531	Silver Dawn Observation
1955	**1535W/509**	**$49.95**
	2243P/C	Santa Fe F3, AB
	6436	Lehigh Valley Hopper
	6462-25	NYC Gondola Car, green
	6468X	Automobile Car, Tuscan
	6257-25	Lionel Caboose, red
1955	**1536W/510**	**$59.95**
	2245P/C	The *Texas Special* F3, AB

Year	Number	Description
	2432	Clifton Vista-Dome
	2432	Clifton Vista-Dome
	2436	Summit Observation
1955	**1539W/513**	**$65.00**
	2243P/C	Santa Fe F3, AB
	3620	Operating Searchlight Car
	6446	N & W Covered Hopper
	6561	Lionel Lines Cable Car
	6560	Lionel Lines Crane Car
	6419	D L & W Work Caboose
1955	**2239W/A-22**	**$55.00**
	2363P/C	Illinois Central F3, AB
	6672	Santa Fe Refrigerator Car
	6464-125	NYC Boxcar
	6414	Evans Auto Loader
	6517	Lionel Lines Bay Window Caboose
1955	**2244W/A-25**	**$65.00**
	2367P/C	Wabash F3, AB
	2530	REA Baggage Car
	2533	Silver Cloud Pullman
	2531	Silver Dawn Observation
1955	**2247W/A-27**	**$65.00**
	2367P/C	Wabash F3, AB
	6462-125	NYC Gondola Car, red
	3662	Operating Milk Car with Platform
	6464-150	Missouri Pacific Boxcar
	3361	Operating Log Car
	6517	Lionel Lines Bay Window Caboose
1956	**1563W/712**	**$67.50**
	2240P/C	Wabash F3, AB
	6467	Miscellaneous Car
	3562-50	Operating Barrel Car, yellow
	3620	Operating Searchlight Car
	6414	Evans Auto Loader
	6357	Lionel Caboose
1956	**1567W/714**	**$75.00**
	2243P/C	Santa Fe F3, AB
	3356	Operating Horse Car with Corral
	3424	Wabash Operating Brakeman Boxcar
	6672	Santa Fe Refrigerator Car
	6430	Cooper-Jarrett Van Car
	6357	Lionel Caboose
1956	**2269W/807**	**$75.00**
	2368P/C	Baltimore & Ohio F3, AB
	3356	Operating Horse Car with Corral
	6518	Transformer Car
	6315	Gulf Chemical Car
	3361	Operating Log Car
	6517	Lionel Lines Bay Window Caboose
1956	**2373W/810**	**$85.00**
	2378P/C	The Milwaukee Road F3, AB
	342	Operating Culvert Loader
	6342	Culvert Car
	3562-50	Operating Barrel Car, yellow
	3662	Operating Milk Car with Platform
	3359	Operating Twin-Bin Dump Car
	6517	Lionel Lines Bay Window Caboose
1957	**2281W/819**	**$62.50**
	2243P/C	Santa Fe F3, AB
	3562-75	Operating Barrel Car, orange
	6464-150	Missouri Pacific Boxcar
	3361	Operating Log Car
	6560	Lionel Lines Crane Car
	6119	D L & W Work Caboose
1957	**2291W/824**	**$81.25**
	2379P/C	Rio Grande F3, AB
	3562-75	Operating Barrel Car, orange
	3530	Operating Generator Car
	3444	Animated Gondola
	6464-525	Minneapolis & St. Louis Boxcar
	6657	Rio Grande Caboose
1957	**2296W/828**	**$100.00**
	2373P/T	Canadian Pacific Twin Diesel F3s, AA
	2552	Skyline 500 Vista-Dome
	2552	Skyline 500 Vista-Dome
	2552	Skyline 500 Vista-Dome
	2551	Banff Park Observation
1958	**2507W**	**$65.00**
	2242P/C	New Haven F3, AB
	3444	Animated Gondola Car
	6464-425	New Haven Boxcar
	6424	Twin Auto Car
	6468-25	New Haven Automobile Car
	6357	Lionel Caboose
1958	**2517W**	**$75.00**
	2379P/C	Rio Grande F3, AB
	6519	Allis Chalmers Car
	6805	Atomic Energy Disposal Car
	6434	Illuminated Poultry Car
	6800	Airplane Car
	6657	Rio Grande Caboose
1958	**2523W**	**$95.00**
	2383P/T	Santa Fe Twin Diesel F3s, AA
	264	Operating Fork Lift Platform Set
	6264	Lumber Car
	6434	Illuminated Poultry Car
	6800	Airplane Car
	3662	Operating Milk Car with Platform
	6517	Lionel Lines Bay Window Caboose
1958	**2526W**	**$100.00**
	2383P/T	Santa Fe Twin Diesel F3s, AA
	2530	REA Baggage Car
	2532	Silver Range Vista-Dome
	2532	Silver Range Vista-Dome
	2531	Silver Dawn Observation
1959	**2537W**	**$75.00**
	2242P/C	New Haven F3, AB
	3435	Operating Aquarium Car
	3650	Searchlight Extension Car
	6464-275	State of Maine Boxcar
	6819	Flat Car with Helicopter
	6427	Lionel Lines Caboose
1959	**2541W**	**$89.95**
	2383P/T	Santa Fe Twin Diesel F3s, AA
	3356	Operating Horse Car with Corral
	3512	Operating Fireman-Ladder Car
	6519	Allis Chalmers Car
	6816	Flat Car with Allis Chalmers Tractor Dozer
	6427	Lionel Lines Caboose
1959, 60	**2544W**	**$100.00, $100.00**
	2383P/T	Santa Fe Twin Diesel F3s, AA
	2530	REA Baggage Car
	2563	Indian Falls Pullman, red stripe
	2562	Regal Pass Vista-Dome, red stripe
	2561	Vista Valley Observation, red stripe

1960	**2555W**	**$150.00**
	2383P/T	Santa Fe Twin Diesel F3s, AA
	3434	Operating Chicken Car with Sweeper
	3366	Operating Circus Car with Matching Corral
	6414	Auto Transport Car
	6464-900	NYC Boxcar
	6357-50	Santa Fe Caboose
	110-85	Trestle Set
	——	Matching Set of Lionel HO Trains
1961	**2574**	**$89.95**
	2383P/T	Santa Fe Twin Diesel F3s, AA
	3665	Minuteman Missile Launching Car
	3419	Operating Helicopter Launching Car
	448	Missile Firing Range Set
	6448	Exploding Target Car
	3830	Operating Submarine Car
	6437	Lionel Lines Caboose
1961	**2576**	**$100.00**
	2383P/T	Santa Fe Twin Diesel F3s, AA
	2563	Indian Falls Pullman
	2562	Regal Pass Vista-Dome
	2562	Regal Pass Vista-Dome
	2561	Vista Valley Observation
1962	**13058**	**$89.95**
	2383P/T	Santa Fe Twin Diesel F3s, AA
	3619	Reconnaissance Copter Car
	3413	Mercury Capsule Launching Car
	6512	Cherry Picker Car
	470	Missile Launching Platform
	6470	Exploding Target Car
	6437	Lionel Lines Caboose
1962	**13088**	**$120.00**
	2383P/T	Santa Fe Twin Diesel F3s, AA
	2523	President Garfield Pullman
	2522	President Harrison Vista-Dome
	2522	President Harrison Vista-Dome
	2521	President McKinley Observation
1963	**13128**	**$89.95**
	2383P/T	Santa Fe Twin Diesel F3s, AA
	3619	Reconnaissance Copter Car
	3413	Mercury Capsule Launching Car
	6512	Cherry Picker Car
	448	Missile Firing Range Set
	6448	Exploding Target Range Car
	6437	Pennsylvania Caboose
1963	**13148**	**$120.00**
	2383	Santa Fe Twin Diesel F3s, AA
	2523	President Garfield Pullman
	2523	President Garfield Pullman
	2522	President Harrison Vista-Dome
	2521	President McKinley Observation
1964	**12720**	**$65.00**
1964, 65, 66	**12730**	**$79.95, $85.00, $90.00**
	2383P/T	Santa Fe Twin Diesel F3s, AA
	6464-725	New Haven Boxcar
	6162-100	Gondola with Canisters, blue
	6414-85	Auto Transport Car, 64
	6414	Auto Transport Car, 65, 66
	6476-135	Lehigh Valley Hopper, yellow
	6437	Pennsylvania Caboose
1964	**12740**	**$79.95**
1964	**12750**	**$95.00**
	2383P/T	Santa Fe Twin-Diesel F3s, AA
	3662	Operating Milk Car with Platform
	6822	Night Crew Searchlight Car
	6361	Timber Car
	6464-525	Minneapolis & St. Louis Boxcar
	6436-110	Lehigh Valley Hopper
	6315-60	Lionel Lines Tank Car
	6437	Pennsylvania Caboose
1964, 65, 66	**12780**	**$120, $125, $125.**
	2383P/T	Santa Fe Twin Diesel F3s, AA
	2523	President Garfield Pullman
	2522	Presdent Harrison Vista-Dome
	2523	President Garfield Pullman
	2521	President McKinley Observation

Uncataloged Sears Set

1956	**9693**	**?**
	2356P/T	Southern Twin Diesel F3s, AA
	2356C	Southern B Unit
	6356	NYC Stock Car
	3484-25	Operating Santa Fe Boxcar
	6464-225	Southern Pacific Boxcar
	6465	Sunoco Oil Car
	6427-1	Lionel Lines Caboose

APPENDIX B: INDIVIDUAL BOXES

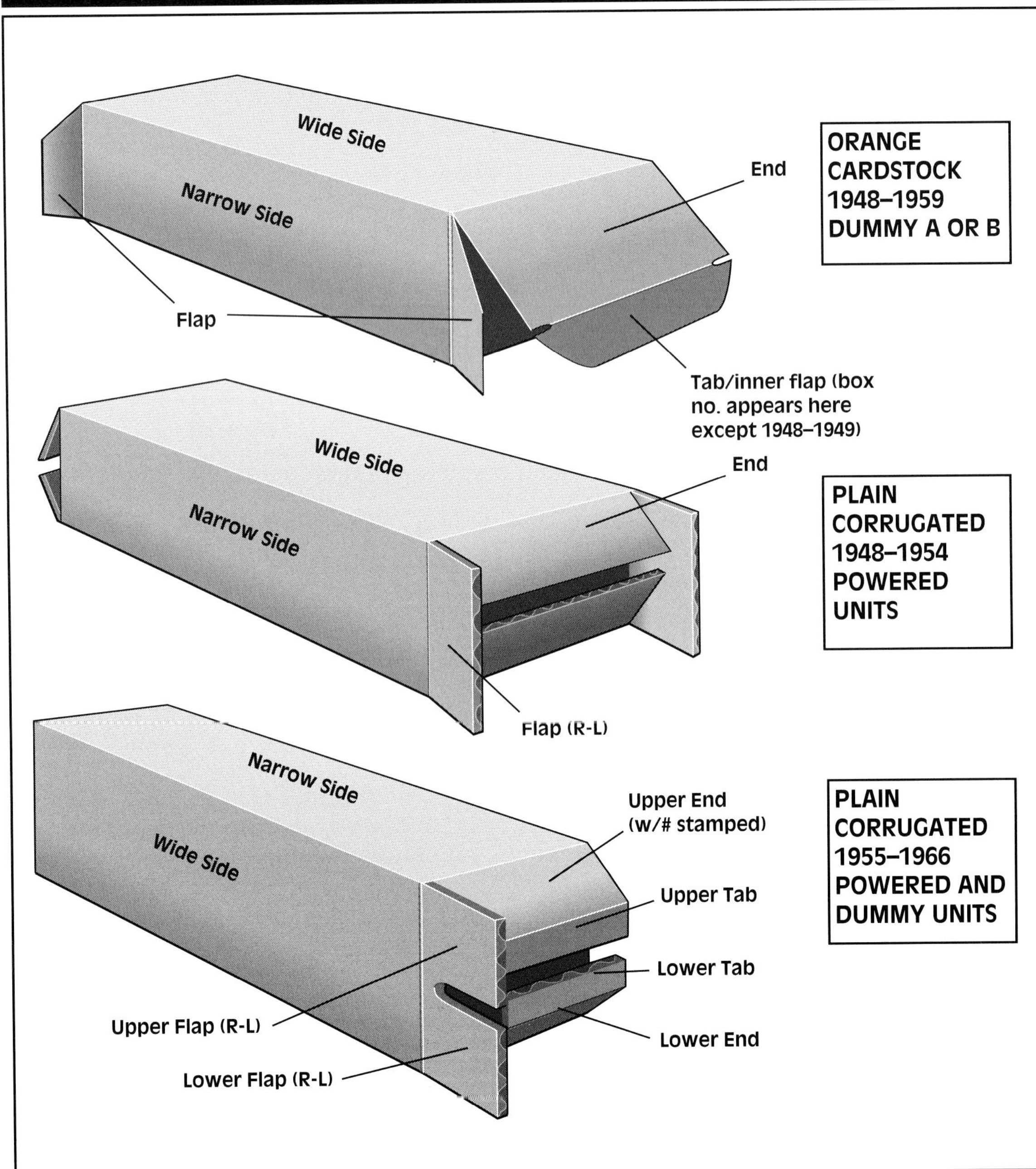

1948 AND 1949 NOMINAL BOX SIZES (BOX DIMENSIONS)

1. Powered Unit Box Size: 3½ x 4¾ x 15¼
2. Dummy (Trailer/Tender) Unit Box Size: 3⅛ x 4⅜ x 15

1948 **2333P: Santa Fe Power Unit**
Box Type: Plain Corrugated "w and w/o" X (targeted for separate sale and goes in master carton)
Manufacturer: Star Corrugated Box Company, Inc., Maspeth, L.I., N.Y.
Box Part Number: 2333P-3 (Vertical Format/Wide Side); 3-30L (Inner Flap)
Date Printed: 1948
Months Printed: None

2333T: Santa Fe Trailer Unit
Box Type: Early Classic
Box Part Number: None

2333P: New York Central Power Unit
Box Type: Plain Corrugated
Manufacturer: Star Corrugated Box Company, Inc.

2333T: New York Central Trailer Unit
Box Type: Early Classic (See box nomenclature on page 80.)
Box Part Number: None

1949 **2333P: Santa Fe Power Unit**
Box Type: Plain Corrugated
Manufacturer: Star Corrugated Box Company, Inc., Maspeth, L.I., N.Y.
Box Part Number: 2333P-3 (Vertical Format); 5-2L (Inner Flap)
Date Printed: None
Months Printed: None

2333T: Santa Fe Trailer Unit
Box Type: Mid-Classic (late 1949), otherwise same as 1948

2333P: New York Central Power Unit
Box Type: Plain Corrugated
Manufacturer: Star Corrugated Box Company, Inc., Maspeth, L.I., N.Y.
Box Part Number: 2334P-3 (Vertical Format); 4 13 L (Inner Flap)
Date Printed: None
Months Printed: None

2333T: New York Central Trailer Unit
Box Type: Mid-Classic (late 1949), otherwise same as 1948

1950 through 1954 NOMINAL BOX SIZES (Box Dimensions)

1. Power Unit Box Size: 3½ x 4¾ x 16½
2. Dummy (Trailer) Unit Box Size: 3 x 4½ x 16¼

3. B Unit Box Size (early 1950): 3¼ x 4¼ x 15
4. B Unit Box Size (1950-1954): 3 x 4¼ x 15

1950 **2343P: Santa Fe Power Unit**
Box Type: Plain Corrugated
Manufacturer: Gair Bogota Corp. (either 2-inch or 3¼-inch seal), Bogota, N.J.
Box Part Number: 2343P-10 Horizontal Format (Wide Side)
Date Printed: None
Months Printed: None

2343T: Santa Fe Trailer Unit
Box Type: Mid-Classic
Inner Flap Number: 2343T-11

2344P: New York Central Power Unit
Box Type: Plain Corrugated
Manufacturer: Gair Bogota Corp. (either 2-inch or 3¼-inch seal), Bogota, N.J.
Box Part Number: 2344P-10 (Outside)
Date Printed: None
Months Printed: None

2344T: New York Central Trailer Unit
Box Type: Mid-Classic
Inner Flap Number: 2344T-11

2343C: Santa Fe B Unit
Box Type: Mid-Classic
Inner Flap Number: 2343-72

2344C: New York Central B Unit
Box Type: Mid-Classic
Inner Flap Number: 2344-60

1951 **2343P: Santa Fe Power Unit**
Box Type: (1) Plain Corrugated
Manufacturer: Kieckhefer Container Co., Delair, N.J.
Box Part Number: 2343P-10 (Vertical Format/Wide Side)
Date Printed: None
Months Printed: None

Box Type: (2) Plain Corrugated
Manufacturer: St. Joe Paper Co. – Container Div., So. Hackensack, N.J.
Box Part Number: 2343P-10 (Vertical Format/Wide Side)
Date Printed: 1951
Months Printed: None/Also 6, 7, 8, 9, 10, 11, 12

2343T: Santa Fe Trailer Unit
Box Type: Same as 1950

2344P: New York Central Power Unit
Box Type: Plain Corrugated
Manufacturer: St. Joe Paper Co. – Container Div., So. Hackensack, N.J.
Box Part Number: 2344P-10
Date Printed: 1951
Months Printed: 6, 7, 8, 9, 10, 11, 12

2344T: New York Central Trailer Unit
Box Type: Same as 1950

2343C: Santa Fe B Unit
Box Type: Mid-Classic
Inner Flap Number: 2343-98

2344C: New York Central B Unit
Box Type: Mid-Classic
Inner Flap Number: 2344-62

1952 **2343P: Santa Fe Power Unit**
Box Type: (1) Plain Corrugated
Manufacturer: National Container Corporation, Long Island City, N.Y.
Box Part Number: 2343P-10 (Vertical Format/Wide Side)
Date Printed: None
Months Printed: None

Box Type: (2) Plain Corrugated
Manufacturer: Gair Bogota Corp., Bogota, N.J.
Box Part Number: 2343P-10 (Vertical Format/Wide Side)
Date Printed: None
Months Printed: None

2343T: Santa Fe Trailer Unit
Box Type: Same as 1950

2344P: New York Central Power Unit
Box Type: Plain Corrugated
Manufacturer: National Container Corporation, Long Island City, N.Y.
Box Part Number: 2344P-10 (Vertical Format/Wide Side)
Date Printed: None
Months Printed: None

2344T: New York Central Trailer Unit
Box Type: Same as 1950

2345P: Western Pacific Power Unit
Box Type: Plain Corrugated
Manufacturer: Densen-Banner Co., Inc., Ridgefield Park, N.J.
Box Part Number: 2345-21 (Vertical Format/Wide Side)
Date Printed: None
Months Printed: None

2345T: Western Pacific Trailer Unit
Box Type: Mid-Classic
Inner Flap Number: 2345-20

2343C: Santa Fe B Unit
Box Type: Same as 1951

Two different 1950 boxes typical for 2343 and 2344. Note horizontal format of printed information on wide side of box.

Note small rubber-stamped letters, perhaps related to inventory control. All four cartons can show up in master cartons.

Early 1950 B-unit box above with wider vertical borders; below, later 1950 version.

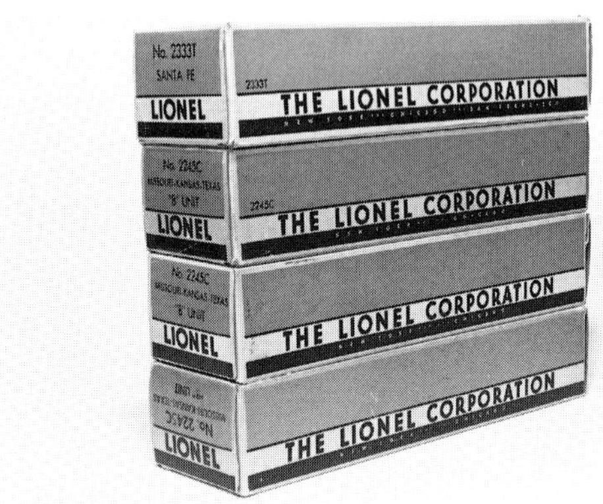

Top box: For comparison purposes
Second: Mid-Classic with 2245-33 inner flap number. Note stock number on side, as on top box.
Third: Late Classic. Note absence of stock number on side.
Bottom: Late Classic bold. Note absence of stock number on side. Two bottom boxes have same 2245-33 number on inner flap.

2344C: New York Central B Unit
Box Type: Same as 1951

1953 **2353P: Santa Fe Power Unit**
Box Type: Plain Corrugated
Manufacturer: St. Joe Paper Co. – Container Div., So. Hackensack, N.J.
Box Part Number: 2353-25 (Vertical Format/Wide Side)
Date Printed: 3
Months Printed: 4, 5, 6, 7, 8, 9, 10, 11, 12; also 2, 3, 4, 5, 6, 7, 8, 9, 10, 11, 12

2353T: Santa Fe Trailer Unit
Box Type: Mid-Classic
Inner Flap Number: 2353-50

2354P: New York Central Power Unit
Box Type: Plain Corrugated
Manufacturer: St. Joe Paper Co. – Container Div., So. Hackensack, N.J.
Box Part Number: 2354-25 (Vertical Format/Wide Side)
Date Printed: 3
Months Printed: 3, 4, 5, 6, 7, 8, 9, 10, 11, 12

2354T: New York Central Trailer Unit
Box Type: Mid-Classic
Inner Flap Number: 2354-50

2355P: Western Pacific Power Unit
Box Type: Plain Corrugated
Manufacturer: St. Joe Paper Co. – Container Div., So. Hackensack, N.J.
Box Part Number: 2355-25 (Vertical Format)
Date Printed: 3
Months Printed: 4, 5, 6, 7, 8, 9, 10, 11, 12

2355T: Western Pacific Trailer Unit
Box Type: Mid-Classic
Inner Flap Number: 2355-50

2343C: Santa Fe B Unit
Box Type: Same as 1951

2344C: New York Central B Unit
Box Type: Same as 1951

1954 **2245P: *Texas Special* Power Unit**
Box Type: Plain Corrugated
Manufacturer: St. Joe Paper Co. – Container Div., So. Hackensack, N.J.
Box Part Number: 2245-30 (Vertical Format/Wide Side)
Date Printed: 4 (Large), 4 (Small)
Months Printed: 7, 8, 9, 10, 11, 12

2245C: *Texas Special* B Unit
Box Type: Mid-Classic
Inner Flap Number: 2245-33

2353P: Santa Fe Power Unit
Box Type: Plain Corrugated
Manufacturer: St. Joe Paper Co. – Container Div., So. Hackensack, N.J.
Box Part Number: 2353-25 (Vertical Format/Wide Side)
Date Printed: 4
Months Printed: 9, 10 11, 12

2353T: Santa Fe Trailer Unit
Box Type: Same as 1953

2354P: New York Central Power Unit
Box Type: Plain Corrugated
Manufacturer: St. Joe Paper Co. – Container Div., So. Hackensack, N.J.
Box Part Number: 2354-25 (Vertical Format/Wide Side)
Date Printed: 4
Months Printed: 8, 9, 10, 11, 12

2354T: New York Central Trailer Unit
Box Type: Same as 1953

2356P: Southern Railway Power Unit
Box Type: Plain Corrugated
Manufacturer: St. Joe Paper Co. – Container Div., So. Hackensack, N.J.
Box Part Number: 2356-26 (Vertical Format/Wide Side)
Date Printed: 4
Months Printed: 7, 8, 9, 10, 11, 12

2356T: Southern Railway Trailer Unit
Box Type: Mid-Classic
Inner Flap Number: 2356-50

2356C: Southern Railway B Unit
Box Type: Mid-Classic
Inner Flap Number: 2356-45

2343C: Santa Fe B Unit
Same as 1951

2344C: New York Central B Unit
Same as 1951

1955 through 1966 NOMINAL BOX SIZES (Box Dimensions)

1. Power Unit Box Size: 3⅛ x 4⅛ x 15¼
2. Dummy (Trailer) Unit Box Size: 3⅛ x 4⅛ x 15¼
3. B Unit Box Size: 3¼ x 4 x 14¼

1955 **2243P: Santa Fe Power Unit**
Box Type: Plain Corrugated
Manufacturer: Express Container Corp., Newark, N.J.
Box Part Number: 2243-15 (Horizontal Format/Wide Side)
Date Printed: None
Months Printed: None

2243C: Santa Fe B Unit
Box Type: Mid-Classic
Inner Flap Number: 2243-12

2245P: *Texas Special* "A" Unit
Same as 1954

2245C: *Texas Special* B Unit
Box Type: Late-Classic & Late-Classic Bold
Inner Flap Number: 2245-33

2343C: Santa Fe B Unit
Same as 1951

2344C: New York Central B Unit
Same as 1951

2353: Santa Fe AA
Same as 1954

2354: New York Central AA
Same as 1954

2356: Southern Railway AA
Same as 1954

2356C: Southern Railway B Unit
Same as 1954

2363P: Illinois Central Power Unit
Box Type: Plain Corrugated
Manufacturer: Express Container Corp., Newark, N.J.
Box Part Number: 2363-17 (Horizontal Format/Wide Side)
Date Printed: None
Months Printed: None

2363C: Illinois Central B Unit
Box Type: Mid-Classic
Miscellaneous: Some have a small rubber-stamped B
Inner Flap Number: 2363-18

2367P: Wabash Power Unit
Box Type: Plain Corrugated
Manufacturer: Express Container Corp., Newark, N.J.
Box Part Number: 2367-15 (Horizontal Format/Wide Side)
Date Printed: None
Months Printed: None

2367C: Wabash B Unit
Box Type: Mid-Classic
Inner Flap Number: 2367-16

1956 **2240P: Wabash Power Unit**
Box Type: Plain Corrugated
Manufacturer: Allcraft Container Corp. Harrison, N.J.
Box Part Number: 2240-15 (Vertical Format/Wide Side)
Date Printed: w & w/o "56"
Months Printed: None

2240C: Wabash B Unit
Box Type: Late Classic
Inner Flap Number: 2240-16

2243P: Santa Fe Power Unit
Box Type: Plain Corrugated
Manufacturer: Allcraft Container Corp., Harrison, N.J.
Box Part Number: 2243-15 (Vertical Format/Wide Side)
Date Printed: 56
Months Printed: None

2243C: Santa Fe B Unit
Box Type: Late Classic
Inner Flap Number: 2243-12

2356: Southern Railway ABA
Same as 1954

2363: Illinois Central AB
Same as 1955

2367: Wabash AB
Same as 1955

2368P: Baltimore & Ohio Power Unit
Box Type: Plain Corrugated
Manufacturer: Allcraft Container Corp., Harrison, N.J.
Box Part Number: 2368-12 (Vertical Format/Wide Side)
Date Printed: 56
Months Printed: None

2368C: Baltimore & Ohio B Unit
Box Type: Late Classic
Inner Flap Number: 2368-18

2378P: Milwaukee Road Power Unit
Box Type: Plain Corrugated
Manufacturer: Allcraft Container Corp., Harrison, N.J.
Box Part Number: 2378-18 (Vertical Format/Wide Side)
Date Printed: 56
Months Printed: None

2378C: Milwaukee Road B Unit
Box Type: Late Classic
Inner Flap Number: 2378-16

1957 **2243P: Santa Fe Power Unit**
Box Type: Plain Corrugated
Manufacturer: Allcraft Container Corp., Harrison, N.J.
Box Part Number: 2243-15 (Vertical Format)
Date Printed: 57
Months Printed: None

2243C: Santa Fe B Unit
Box Type: Same as 1956

2373P: Canadian Pacific Power Unit
Box Type: Plain Corrugated
Manufacturer: Express Container Corp.,Newark, N.J.
Box Part Number: 2373-11 (Horizontal Format/Wide Side)
Date Printed: None
Months Printed: None

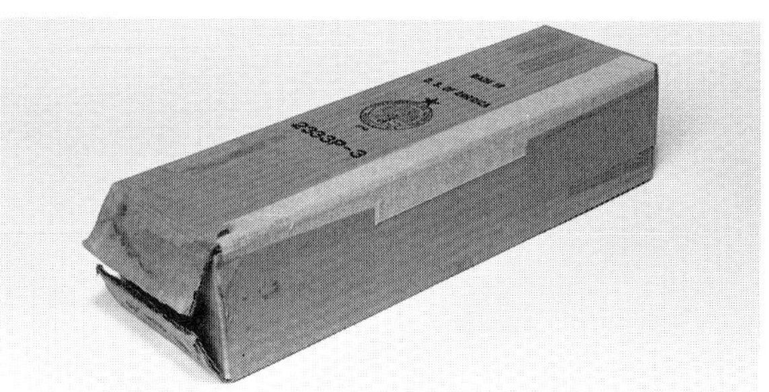

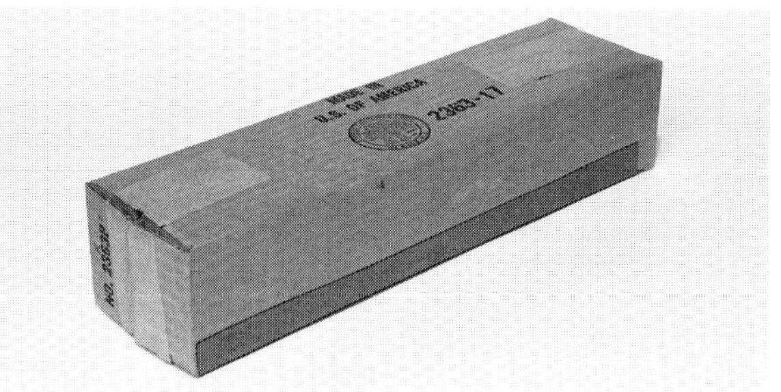

Top: 1948/49 style (vertical format)
Second: 1955-style (horizontal format)
Third: 1958-style (vertical format)
Bottom: 1959–1962 (horizontal format)

2373T: Canadian Pacific Trailer Unit
Box Type: Plain Corrugated
Manufacturer: National Container Corporation, Long Island City, N.Y.
Box Part Number: 2373-27 (Horizontal Format/Wide Side)

2379P: Rio Grande Power Unit
Box Type: Plain Corrugated
Manufacturer: Express Container Corp., Newark, N.J.
Box Part Number: 2379-11 (Horizontal Format/Wide Side)
Date Printed: None
Months Printed: None

2379C B Unit
Box Type: Late Classic
Inner Flap Number: 2379-54

1958 **2242P: New Haven Power Unit**
Box Type: Plain Corrugated
Manufacturer: Star Corrugated Box Company, Inc., Maspeth, L.I., N.Y.
Box Part Number: 2242-15 (Vertical Format/Narrow Side)
Date Printed: None
Months Printed: None

2242C: New Haven B Unit
Box Type: Late Classic
Inner Flap Number: 2242-53

2379 Rio Grande, AB
Same as 1957

2383P: Santa Fe Power Unit
Box Type: Plain Corrugated
Manufacturer: Star Corrugated Box Company, Inc., Maspeth, L.I., N.Y.
Box Part Number: 2383-11 (Vertical Format/ Narrow Side)
Date Printed: None
Months Printed: None

2383T: Santa Fe Trailer Unit
Box Type: Plain Corrugated
Manufacturer: Star Corrugated Box Company, Inc., Maspeth, L.I., N.Y.
Box Part Number: 2383-12 (Vertical Format/Narrow Side)
Date Printed: None
Months Printed: None

1959 **2242: New Haven AB**
Same as 1958 (?)

383P: Santa Fe Power Unit
Box Type: Plain Corrugated/w Perforated Side Panel
Manufacturer: (Type I) Mead Containers (Horizontal Format/Narrow Side), North Bergen, N.J.
Inner Flap Number: 2383-11: (NOTE CHANGE FROM OUTSIDE TO INNER FLAP)
Date Printed: None
Months Printed: None

2383T: Santa Fe Trailer Unit
Box Type: Plain Corrugated/w Perforated Side Panel
Manufacturer: (Type I) Mead Containers (Horizontal Format/Narrow Side) North Bergen, N.J.
Inner Flap Number: 2383-12
Date Printed: None
Months Printed: None

1960 **2383P: Santa Fe Power Unit**
Same as 1959

2383T: Santa Fe Trailer Unit
Same as 1959

1961 **2383P: Santa Fe Power Unit**
Same as 1959

2383T: Santa Fe Trailer Unit
Same as 1959

1962 **2383P: Santa Fe Power Unit**
Same as 1959

2383T: Santa Fe Trailer Unit
Same as 1959

2383P: Santa Fe Power Unit
Box Type: Plain Corrugated (NOTE: NO LONGER PERFORATED)
Manufacturer: (Type II) Mead Containers (Vertical Format/Narrow Side), North Bergen, N.J.
Inner Flap Number: 2383-11
Date Printed: None
Months Printed: None

2383T: Santa Fe Trailer Unit
Box Type: Plain Corrugated
Manufacturer: (Type II) Mead Containers (Vertical Format/Narrow Side), North Bergen, N.J.
Inner Flap Number: 2383-11
Date Printed: None
Months Printed: None

1963 **2383P: Santa Fe Power Unit**
Same as 1962 (Type II Mead Containers)

2383T: Santa Fe Trailer Unit
Same as 1962 (Type II Mead Containers)

2383P: Santa Fe Power Unit
Box Type: Plain Corrugated (NOTE: BOX PART NUMBER RETURNED)
Manufacturer: (Type III) Mead Containers, North Bergen, N.J.
Box Part Number: 2383-11 (Horizontal Format/Narrow Side)
Date Printed: None
Months Printed: None

2383T: Santa Fe Trailer Unit
Box Type: Plain Corrugated (NOTE: BOX PART NUMBER RETURNED)
Manufacturer: (Type III) Mead Containers, North Bergen, N.J.
Box Part Number: 2383-12 (Vertical Format/Narrow Side)
Date Printed: None
Months Printed: None

1964 **2383P: Santa Fe Power Unit**
Box Type: Plain Corrugated
Manufacturer: (Type III) Mead Containers, North Bergen, N.J.
Box Part Number: 2383-11 (Horizontal Format/Narrow Side)
Date Printed: None
Months Printed: None

2383T: Santa Fe Trailer Unit
Box Type: Plain Corrugated
Manufacturer: (Type III) Mead Containers, North Bergen, N.J.
Box Part Number: 2383-12 (Vertical Format/ Narrow Side)
Date Printed: None
Months Printed: None

1965 **2383P: Santa Fe Power Unit**
Same as 1964

2383T: Santa Fe Trailer Unit
Same as 1964

1966 **2383P: Santa Fe Power Unit**
Same as 1964

2383T: Santa Fe Trailer Unit
Same as 1964

NOTE: Star Corrugated boxes were also used during 1959 production. From 1963 through 1966 there was a mixed usage of non-perforated boxes (possibly introduced in late 1962). Also, some later boxes had a bolder box number than earlier ones. Individual boxes for 1964 separate sale are sometimes Type II Mead boxes.

APPENDIX C: MASTER CARTONS

By Frank and Manny Piazza and Dan Mega

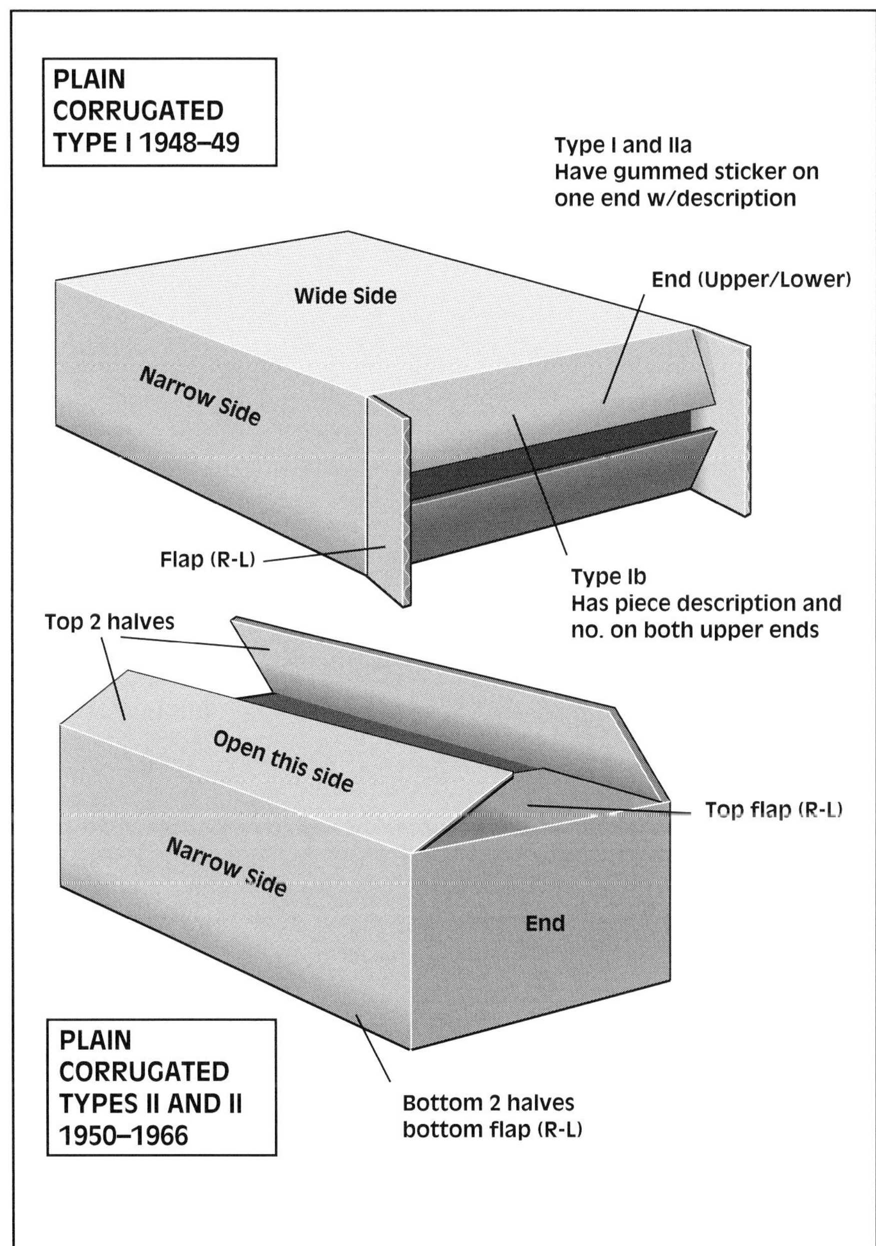

TYPE I: 1948, 7 x 16 x 5, and description, plain corrugated, with black letterpress certificate and rubber-stamped catalog item number. Carton was sealed using art deco-style tape, and covered with an orange and blue letterpress gummed label.

TYPE Ia: 1949, 7 x 16 x 5, and description (early), same as Type I, except the certificate size was enlarged, and the date, 1949, was included in the same typeface.

TYPE Ib: 1949, 7 x 16 x 5, and description (late), plain corrugated with black letterpress certificate and rubber-stamped box number, with black letterpress description on end flaps. (SP/BW). Carton was closed/sealed using plain gummed tape.

TYPE II: 1950, 7 x 17 x 5½, description, plain corrugated with blue letterpress certificate and box number. Box ends with orange field (actually printed first) with a blue border and lettering. Note: Box transition to both a top and bottom opening, instead of at each end, to accommodate the new packaging process.

TYPE IIa: 1952, 7 x 17 x 5½, description, plain corrugated with blue letterpress certificate and box number. Box ends with blue border and lettering, which also included OPS information, one side only, with rubber-stamped (OPS-SR4-CPR7). Note: Transition of box ends from orange and blue to a single color process. (SP/BW).

TYPE IIb: 1953, 7 x 17 x 5½, description, same as Type IIa, except absence of OPS data, which caused a change in the size/shape of the printing. (SP/BW)

TYPE IIc: 1954, 7 x 17 x 5½, description, plain corrugated with blue letterpress certificate on bottom of the box, instead of the side. Box ends with cataloged product identification in red print and blue reversed manufacturer's name. Box Sides with red circle L, and manufacturer's name and location in blue. Note transition: Box number moved to inside inner flap.

TYPE III: 1955, 7 x 15¾ x 4⅝, same as Type IIc, except size proportions of type are smaller, because of a scaled-down box size.

TYPE IIIa: 56–57, 7 x 15¾ x 4⅝, description, same as Type III, except artwork done to the bottom and sides of the box changes, because of change in vendors. (SP/BW)

TYPE IIIb: 1958–1966, 7 x 15¾ x 4⅝, description, same as Type IIIa, except no Magnetraction R in red, and flap and outside box number.

NOTE: Research on Postwar Lionel Trains is an on-going affair. If you have any information on an item we may have left out, or needs to be corrected, please let us know. A photo of the item would be appreciated.

Left to right: 1948 – note stock number and smaller manufacturer's certificate; 1949 – larger manufacturer's certificate and date; 1949 – suffix 161 added.

1948 **2333 Santa Fe, AA (note size of Certificate of Box Maker)**
Box Type: I
Manufacturer: Star Corrugated Box Company, Inc., Maspeth, L.I., N.Y.
Box Part Number: 2333 (Outside); 10-1C (Inner Flap)
Date Printed: None
Months Printed: None
Box Dimensions: 7 x 16 x 5

2333 New York Central, AA
Box Type: I
Manufacturer: Star Corrugated Box Company, Inc., Maspeth, L.I., N.Y.
Box Part Number:
Date Printed:
Months Printed:
Box Dimensions: 7 x 16 x 5

1949 **2333 Santa Fe, AA (note size of Certificate of Box Maker)**
Box Type: Ia
Manufacturer: Star Corrugated Box Company, Inc., Maspeth, L.I., N.Y.
Box Part Number: 2333 (Outside); 4-13L and 4-29C (Inner Flap)
Date Printed: 1949
Months Printed: None
Box Dimensions: 7 x 16 x 5

2333 Santa Fe, AA
Box Type: Ib
Manufacturer: Star Corrugated Box Company, Inc., Maspeth, L.I., N.Y.
Box Part Number: 2333-161
Date Printed: 1949
Months Printed: None
Box Dimensions: 7 x 16 x 5

2333 New York Central, AA
Box Type (1): Ia
Manufacturer: Star Corrugated Box Company, Inc., Maspeth, L.I., N.Y.
Box Part Number: 2333 (Outside); 4-5L (Inner Flap)
Date Printed: 1949
Months Printed: None
Box Dimensions: 7 x 16 x 5

2333 New York Central, AA
Box Type (2): Ib
Manufacturer: Star Corrugated Box Company, Inc., Maspeth, L.I., N.Y.
Box Part Number: 2334-26
Date Printed: 1949
Months Printed: None
Box Dimensions: 7 x 16 x 5

1950 **2343 Santa Fe, AA**
Box Type: II
Manufacturer: Star Corrugated Box Company, Inc., Maspeth, L.I., N.Y.
Box Part Number: 2343-12 (Outside)
Date Printed: 1950
Months Printed: None
Box Dimensions: 7 x 17 x 5½

2344 New York Central, AA
Box Type: II
Manufacturer: Star Corrugated Box Company, Inc., Maspeth, L.I., N.Y.
Box Part Number: 2344-12 (Outside)
Date Printed: 1950
Months Printed: None
Box Dimensions: 7 x 17 x 5½

1951 **2343 Santa Fe, AA: Not Available**
2344 New York Central, AA: Not Available

1952 **2343 Santa Fe, AA**
Box Type: IIa
Manufacturer: Star Corrugated Box Company, Inc., Maspeth, L.I., N.Y.
Box Part Number: 2343-12 (Outside)
Date Printed: None
Months Printed: None
Box Dimensions: 7 x 17 x 5½

2344 New York Central, AA
Box Type: IIa
Manufacturer: Star Corrugated Box Company, Inc., Maspeth, L.I., N.Y.
Box Part Number: 2344-12
Date Printed: None
Months Printed: None
Box Dimensions: 7 x 17 x 5½

2345 Western Pacific, AA
Box Type: IIa
Manufacturer: Densen Banner Co., Ridgefield Park, N.J.
Box Part Number: 2345-22
Date Printed: None
Months Printed: None
Box Dimensions: 7 x 17 x 5½

1953 **2353 Santa Fe, AA**
Box Type: IIb
Manufacturer: Star Corrugated Box Company, Inc. Maspeth, L.I., N.Y.
Box Part Number: 2353-51
Date Printed: None
Months Printed: None
Box Dimensions: 7 x 17 x 5½

2354 New York Central, AA
Box Type:
Manufacturer:
Box Part Number:
Date Printed:
Months Printed:
Box Dimensions:

2355 Western Pacific, AA
Box Type: IIb
Manufacturer: National Container Corporation Long Island City, N.Y.
Box Part Number: 2355-51
Date Printed: None
Months Printed: None
Box Dimensions: 7 x 17 x 5½

1954 **2245 *Texas Special*, AB**
Box Type: Plain w/Blue & Red Print and Circle L
Manufacturer: Densen Banner Co. Ridgefield Park, N.J.
Box Part Number: 2245-31
Date Printed: 7-54
Months Printed: None
Box Dimensions: 7 x 17 x 5½

2353 Santa Fe, AA
Box Type: Type IIc
Manufacturer: Star Corrugated Box Company, Inc., Maspeth, L.I., N.Y.
Box Part Number: 10-22D (Outside); 2353-51 (Inner Flap)
Date Printed: None
Months Printed: None
Box Dimensions: 7 x 17 x 5½

2354 New York Central, AA
Box Type: IIc
Manufacturer: St. Joe Paper Co. – Container Div., So. Hackensack, N.J.
Box Part Number: 2354-51
Date Printed: 4
Months Printed: 10, 11, 12...and 7, 8, 9, 10, 11, 12
Box Dimensions: 7 x 17 x 5½

2356 Southern, AA
Box Type: IIc
Manufacturer: Star Corrugated Box Company, Inc. Maspeth, L.I., N.Y.
Box Part Number: 2356-54
Date Printed: None
Months Printed: None
Box Dimensions: 7 x 17 x 5½

1955 **2243 Santa Fe, AB**
Box Type:
Manufacturer:
Box Part Number:
Date Printed:
Months Printed:
Box Dimensions:

2245 *Texas Special*, AB
Box Information: Same as 1954

2353 Santa Fe, AA
Box Information: Same as 1954

2354 New York Central, AA
Box Information: Same as 1954

2356 Southern, AA
Box Type: IIc
Manufacturer: St. Joe Paper Co. – Container Div., So. Hackensack, N.J.
Box Part Number: 2356-?
Date Printed: 5
Months Printed: 4, 5, 6, 7, 8, 9, 10, 11, 12
Box Dimensions: 7 x 17 x 5½

2363 Illinois Central, AB
Box Type: III
Manufacturer: Schiffenhaus Bros., Newark, N.J.
Box Part Number: 2363-184
Date Printed: 1955
Months Printed: None
Box Dimensions: 7 x 15¾ x 4⅝

2367 Wabash, AB
Box Type: III
Manufacturer: Schiffenhaus Bros., Newark, N.J.
Box Part Number: 2367-190
Date Printed: 1955
Months Printed: 2 + 2 Dots
Box Dimensions: 7 x 15¾ x 4⅝

1956 **2240 Wabash, AB**
Box Type: Type IIIa
Manufacturer: St. Joe Paper Co. – Container Div., So. Hackensack, N.J.
Box Part Number: 2240-32
Date Printed: 6
Months Printed: 10, 11, 12
Box Dimensions: 7 x 15¾ x 4⅝

2243 Santa Fe, AB
Box Type: IIIa
Manufacturer: St. Joe Paper Co. – Container Div., So. Hackensack, N.J.
Box Part Number: 2243-203
Date Printed: 6
Months Printed: 10, 11, 12
Box Dimensions: 7 x 15¾ x 4⅝

2356 Southern, AA
Box Information: Same as 1954/1955

2363 Illinois Central, AB
Box Information: Same as 1955

2367 Wabash, AB
Box Information: Same as 1955

2368 Baltimore & Ohio, AB
Box Type: IIIa
Manufacturer: St. Joe Paper Co. – Container Div., So. Hackensack, N.J.
Box Part Number: 2368-13
Date Printed: 6
Months Printed: 9, 10, 11, 12
Box Dimensions: 7 x 15¾ x 4⅝

2378 Milwaukee Road, AB
Box Type: Plain Corrugated
Manufacturer: St. Joe Paper Co. – Container Div., So. Hackensack, N.J.
Box Part Number: 2378-19
Date Printed: 6
Months Printed: 10, 11, 12
Box Dimensions: 7 x 15¾ x 4⅝

1957 **2243 Santa Fe, AB**
Box Type: IIIa
Manufacturer: St. Joe Paper Co. – Container Div., So. Hackensack, N.J.
Box Part Number: 2243-203
Date Printed: 7
Months Printed: 8, 9, 10, 11, 12
Box Dimensions: 7 x 15¾ x 4⅝

**Top: 1958 master carton 2383.
Bottom: Typical of 1960s, generic box with rubber-stamped number.**

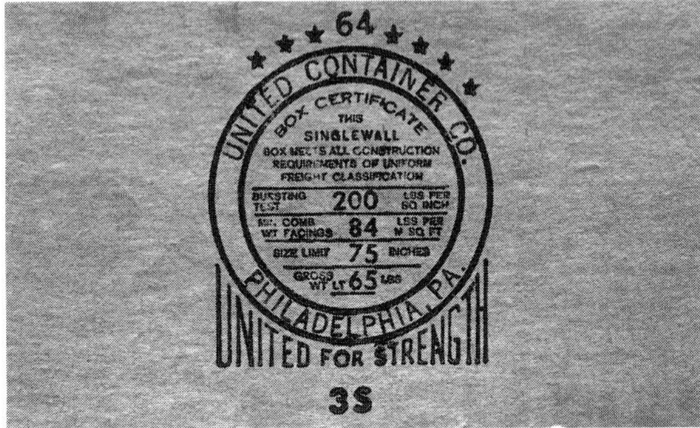

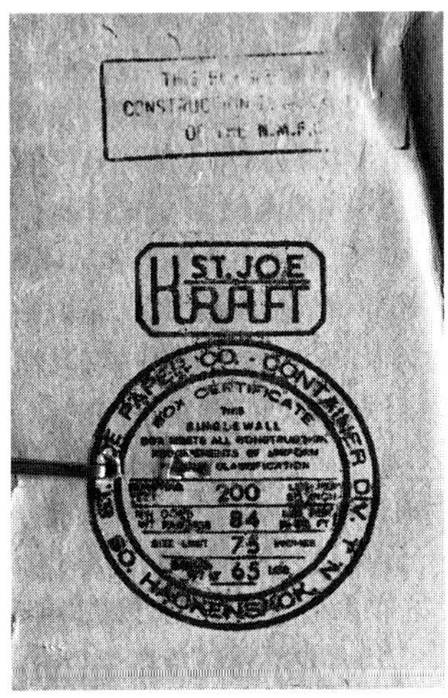

Manufacturer Box Certificates. Top: 1963 master carton. Middle: 1964 master carton. Bottom: 1965 master carton.

2379 Rio Grande, AB
Box Type: IIIa
Manufacturer: St. Joe Paper Co. – Container Div., So. Hackensack, N.J.
Box Part Number: 2379-12
Date Printed: 7
Months Printed: 8, 9, 10, 11, 12
Box Dimensions: 7 x 15¾ x 4⅝

2373 Canadian Pacific, AA
Box Type: IIIa
Manufacturer: Gibraltar Corrugated Paper Co. North Bergen, N.J.
Box Part Number: 2373-40
Date Printed: None
Months Printed: None
Box Dimensions: 7 x 15¾ x 4⅝

1958 **2242 New Haven, AB**
Box Type: IIIb
Manufacturer: St. Joe Paper Co. – Container Div., So. Hackensack, N.J.
Box Part Number: 2242-16
Date Printed: 8
Months Printed: 8, 9, 10, 11, 12
Box Dimensions: 7 x 15¾ x 4⅝

2379 Rio Grande, AB
Box Information: Same as 1957

2383 Santa Fe, AA
Box Type: IIIb
Manufacturer: St. Joe Paper Co. – Container Div., So. Hackensack, N.J.
Box Part Number: 2383-13
Date Printed: 8
Months Printed: 9, 10, 11, 12
Box Dimensions: 7 x 15¾ x 4⅝

1959 **2242 New Haven, AB**
Box Information: Same as 1958

2383 Santa Fe, AA
Box Information: Same as 1958
NOTE: An all-yellow corrugated master carton (1959) for the 2383 Santa Fe has been reported; however, no other details or descriptions of this box are available.

1960 **2383 Santa Fe, AA**
Box Type: IIIb

1961 **2383 Santa Fe, AA**
Box Type: IIIb

1962 **2383 Santa Fe, AA**
Box Type: IIIb

1963 **2383 Santa Fe, AA**
Box Type: IIIb
Manufacturer: United Container Co., Philadelphia, Pa.
Box Part Number: 12-94
Date Printed: *** 63 ****
Months Printed: Not Shown.....3 S
Box Dimensions: 7 x 15¾ x 4⅝

1964 **2383 Santa Fe, AA**
Box Type: IIIb
Manufacturer: United Container Co. Philadelphia, Pa.
Box Part Number: 12-94
Date Printed: *** 64 ****
Months Printed: Not Shown.....3 S
Box Dimensions: 7 x 15¾ x 4⅝

1965 **2383 Santa Fe, AA**
Box Type: IIIb
Manufacturer: St. Joe Paper Co. – Container Div., So. Hackensack, N.J.
Box Part Number: 12-94
Date Printed: None
Months Printed: None
Box Dimensions: 7 x 15¾ x 4⅝

1966 **2383 Santa Fe, AA**
Box Type: IIIb
Manufacturer: Mead Containers, North Bergen, N. J.
Box Part Number: 12-94
Date Printed: None
Months Printed: None
Box Dimensions: 7 x 15¾ x 4⅝

APPENDIX D: SET BOXES

Information provided is based on observed samples only. Conclusions can be drawn by logic where samples were not observed. Nominal box sizes are listed. All boxes are corrugated. In many cases the box part no. is shown on the glued-down underside of an inside flap, making inspection impossible without damaging the box. This accounts for question marks in the listings or "none" or "not shown."

1948 F3 SETS

2133W 2333 Santa Fe, AA 4 car freight 65.00
Box Type:
Box Manufacturer:
Date Printed:
Months Printed:
Box Part Number:
Box Dimensions:

2133W 2333 NYC, AA 4 car freight 65.00
Box Type:
Box Manufacturer:
Date Printed:
Months Printed:
Box Part Number:
Box Dimensions:

1949 F3 SETS

2151W 2333 Santa Fe, AA 5 car freight 67.50
Box Type: Plain w/orange and blue label
Box Manufacturer: Gair Bogota Corp., Bogota, N.J.
Date Printed: Not Shown
Months Printed: Not Shown
Box Part Number: 2151 W-1
Box Dimensions: 15¾ x 15½ x 7

2151W 2333 NYC, AA 5 car freight 67.50
Box Type: Plain w/orange and blue label
Box Manufacturer: Gair Bogota Corporation, Bogota, N.J.
Date Printed: Not Shown
Months Printed: Not Shown
Box Part Number: 2151W-1
Box Dimensions: 15¾ x 15½ x 7

1950 F3 SETS

2161W 2343 Santa Fe, AA 5 car freight 67.50
Box Type: Plain w/orange and blue letterpress label & $
Box Manufacturer: Gair Bogota Corporation, Bogota, N.J.
Date Printed: Not Shown
Months Printed: Not Shown
Box Part Number: 2161W-1
Box Dimensions: 13½ x 17 x 7

2171W 2344 NYC, AA 5 car freight 67.50
Box Type: Plain w/orange and blue letterpress label
Box Manufacturer: Gair Bogota Corporation, Bogota, N.J.
Date Printed: Not Shown
Months Printed: Not Shown
Box Part Number: 2171W-1
Box Dimensions: 13½ x 17 x 7

2175W (1) 2343 Santa Fe, AA 5 car freight 57.50
Box Type: Plain w/orange and blue letterpress label w/$57.50
Box Manufacturer: Gair Bogota Corporation, Bogota, N.J.
Date Printed: Not Shown
Months Printed: Not Shown
Box Part Number: 2175W-1
Box Dimensions: 13½ x 17 x 7

2175W (2) 2343 Santa Fe, AA 5 car freight 57.50
Box Type: Plain w/orange and blue letterpress label/ "No" $57.50
Box Manufacturer: Kieckhefer Container Co., Delair, N.J.
Date Printed: Not Shown
Months Printed: Not Shown
Box Part Number: 2175W-1
Box Dimensions: 13½ x 17 x 7

2185W 2344 NYC, AA 5 car freight 57.50
Box Type: Plain cor w/orange and blue letterpress label & $
Box Manufacturer: Gair Bogota Corporation, Bogota, N.J.
Date Printed: Not Shown
Months Printed: Not Shown
Box Part Number: 2185W-1
Box Dimensions: 13½ x 17 x 7

1951 F3 SETS

2175W (1) 2343 Santa Fe, AA 5 car freight 70.00
Box Type: Plain w/orange and blue letterpress label w/ OPS Sticker
Box Manufacturer: Kieckhefer Container Co., Delair, N.J.
Date Printed: Not Shown
Months Printed. Not Shown
Box Part Number: 2175W-1
Box Dimensions: 13½ x 17 x 7

2175W (2) 2343 Santa Fe, AA 5 car freight 70.00
Box Type: Plain w/blue print
Box Manufacturer: Star Corrugated Box Company, Inc., Maspeth, L.I., N.Y.
Date Printed: Not Shown
Months Printed: Not Shown
Box Part Number: 2175W-1
Box Dimensions: 13½ x 17 x 7

2185W 2344 NYC, AA 5 car freight 70.00
Box Type:
Box Manufacturer:
Date Printed:
Months Printed:
Box Part Number:
Box Dimensions:

Three styles of set boxes
Top: 1950 with price preprinted and orange border and blue letterpress label
Middle: 1951, same box, same label, but with OPS sticker
Bottom: 1951, plain corrugated with blue type

1952 F3 SETS

2191W 2343 Santa Fe, ABA 4 car freight 70.00
Box Type: Plain w/OPS printed
Box Manufacturer: Star Corrugated Box Company, Inc., Maspeth, L.I., N.Y.

Date Printed: 52
Months Printed: Not Shown
Box Part Number: ?
Box Dimensions: 13½ x 17 x 7

2190W 2343 Santa Fe, AA 4 car pass. 89.50
Box Type: Plain w/blue printing & OPS printed
Box Manufacturer: Star Corrugated Box Company, Inc., Maspeth, L.I., N.Y.
Date Printed: Not Shown
Months Printed: Not Shown
Box Part Number: 2190-W-1 (Outside and Inner Flap)
Box Dimensions: 13 x 21½ x 8

2193W 2344 NYC, ABA 4 car freight 70.00
Box Type: Plain w/OPS printed/w/o OPS
Box Manufacturer: St. Joe Paper Co. – Container Div., So. Hackensack, N.J.
Date Printed: 1952 (both)
Months Printed: 7, 8, 9, 10, 11, 12 and 9, 10, 11, 12
Box Part Number: 2193W-?
Box Dimensions: 13½ x 17 x 7

1953 F3 SETS

2207W 2353 Santa Fe, ABA 4 car freight 70.00
Box Type: Plain
Box Manufacturer: Denson Banner Co., Ridgefield Park, N.J.
Date Printed: 53
Months Printed: Not Shown
Box Part Number: 2207W-1
Box Dimensions: 13½ x 17 x 8

2209W 2354 NYC, ABA 4 car freight 70.00
Box Type: Plain
Box Manufacturer: Densen Banner Co., Ridgefield Park, N.J.
Date Printed: 6 53
Months Printed: Not Shown
Box Part Number: ?
Box Dimensions: 13½ x 17 x 8

2190W 2353 Santa Fe, AA 4 car pass. 89.50
Box Type: Plain; no OPS
Box Manufacturer: Densen Banner Co., Ridgefield Park, N.J.
Date Printed: Not Shown
Months Printed: Not Shown
Box Part Number: 2190W1. No spaces or hyphens between numbers. (See 1952 listing also.)
Box Dimensions: 13 x 21½ x 8

1954 F3 SETS

1517W 2245 *Texas Special* AB 4 car freight 59.95
Box Type: Plain outfit box with circle L
Box Manufacturer: Star Corrugated Box Company, Inc., Maspeth., L.I., N.Y.
Date Printed: Not Shown
Months Printed: Not Shown
Box Part Number: 1517-1
Box Dimensions: 12 x 17 x 7

1520W 2245 *Texas Special*, AB 3 car pass. 69.50
Box Type: Plain outfit box with circle L
Box Manufacturer: Star Corrugated Box Company, Inc., Maspeth., L.I., N.Y.
Date Printed: Not Shown
Months Printed: Not Shown
Box Part Number: 1520W-1
Box Dimensions: 11¼ x 19 x 7¼

2227W 2353 Santa Fe, AA 5 car freight 69.50
Box Type: Plain outfit box
Box Manufacturer: Star Corrugated Box Company, Inc. Maspeth., L.I., N.Y.
Date Printed: Not Shown
Months Printed: Not Shown
Box Part Number: 2227W-1
Box Dimensions: 13¾ x 17½ x 8

2229W 2354 NYC, AA 5 car freight 69.50
Box Type:
Box Manufacturer:
Date Printed:
Months Printed:
Box Part Number:
Box Dimensions:

2231W (2) 2356 Southern, ABA 5 car freight 79.50
Box Type: Plain w/red and blue print and circle L
Box Manufacturer: St. Joe Paper Co. – Container Div., So. Hackensack, N.J.
Date Printed: 4 (#4 is also on Shipping Carton w/7-12 months)
Months Printed: Box (1) 7,8,9,10,11,12; Box (2) 8,9,10,11,12
Box Part Number: 2231W-1; 2231W-2
Box Dimensions: 13½ x 17¼ x 9; SC 14 x 17½ x 18¾

2234W 2353 Santa Fe, AA 4 car pass. 89.50
Box Type: Plain w/red and blue print and circle L
Box Manufacturer: St. Joe Paper Co. – Container Div., So. Hackensack, N.J.
Date Printed: 4
Months Printed: 9, 10, 11, 12
Box Part Number: 2234W-1
Box Dimensions: 13 x 21½ x 7¼

1955 F3 SETS

1535W 2243 Santa Fe, AB 4 car freight 49.95
Box Type: Plain with circle L
Box Manufacturer: Express Container Corp.,Newark, N.J.
Date Printed: Not Shown
Months Printed: Not Shown
Box Part Number: 55-81; 55-36
Box Dimensions: 10½ x 18¼ x 7; 11 x 18½ x 7¾

1536W 2245 *Texas Special*, AB 3 car pass. 59.95
Box Type: Plain/1955 Outfit
Box Manufacturer: St. Joe Paper Co. – Container Div., So. Hackensack, N.J.
Date Printed: 5
Months Printed: 4, 5, 6, 7, 8, 9, 10, 11, 12
Box Part Number: 55-41 (Inside "small" flap)
Box Dimensions: 11 x 19 x 7¼

1539W 2243 Santa Fe, AB 5 car freight 65.00
Box Type: Plain/1955 Outfit/paste-on sticker
Box Manufacturer: National Container Corporation, Long Island City, N.Y.
Date Printed: 55
Months Printed: Not Shown (5 dots)
Box Part Number: 55-58
Box Dimensions: 14½ x 16½ x 7

2239W 2363 Illinois Central, AB 4 car freight 55.00
Box Type: Plain w/blue and red letter and circle L
Box Manufacturer: National Container Corporation Long Island City, N.Y.
Date Printed: 55 .... (4 dots)
Months Printed: Not Shown
Box Part Number: 55-81 (Inner Flap)
Box Dimensions: 11¾ x 20½ x 6½

2244W 2367 Wabash, AB 3 car pass. 65.00
Box Type: Plain w/"1955 Outfit"
Box Manufacturer: St. Joe Paper Co. – Container Div., So. Hackensack, N.J.
Date Printed: 5
Months Printed: 9, 10, 11, 12
Box Part Number: 55-96 (Inner small flap)
Box Dimensions: 13 x 18¼ x 7½

2247W 2367 Wabash, AB 5 car freight 65.00
Box Type: Plain/1955 Outfit
Box Manufacturer: Kieckhefer Container Co., Delair, N.J.
Date Printed: Not Shown
Months Printed: Not Shown
Box Part Number: 55-106 (Both Flaps)
Box Dimensions: 13¾ x 18¾ x 7

1956 F3 SETS

1563W 2240 Wabash, AB 5 car freight 67.50
Box Type: Line pattern box
Box Manufacturer: St. Joe Paper Co. – Container Div., So. Hackensack, N.J.
Date Printed: 6
Months Printed: 9, 10, 11, 12
Box Part Number: ?
Box Dimensions: 12¼ x 18¼ x 7¾

714/1567W 2243 Santa Fe, AB 5 car freight 75.00
Box Type: Line pattern box
Box Manufacturer: Gibraltar Corrugated Paper Co., Inc., North Bergen, N.J.
Date Printed: Not Shown
Months Printed: Not Shown
Box Part Number: None
Box Dimensions: 14½ x 18½ x 7¾

2269W **2368 Balt & Ohio, AB** **5 car freight** **75.00**
Box Type: Line pattern box
Box Manufacturer: Gibraltar Corrugated Paper Co., Inc., North Bergen, N.J.
Date Printed: Not Shown
Months Printed: Not Shown
Box Part Number: ?
Box Dimensions: 13¼ x 20 x 8

2273W **2378 Milwaukee Road, AB** **5 car frt/Acc** **85.00**
Box Type: Plain
Box Manufacturer: St. Joe Paper Co. – Container Div., So. Hackensack, N.J.
Date Printed: 6
Months Printed: 10, 11, 12
Box Part Number: Not Shown
Box Dimensions: 15½ x 18½ x 10½

9693 **2356 Southern, ABA** **5 car freight** **?**
Box Type: Plain
Box Manufacturer: St. Joe Paper Co. – Container Div., So. Hackensack, N.J.
Date Printed: 6
Months Printed: 5, 6, 7, 8, 9, 10, 11, 12
Box Part Number: Not Shown
Box Dimensions: 14½ x 19 x 7½

1957 F3 SETS

2281W **2243 Santa Fe, AB** **5 car freight** **62.50**
Box Type: Line pattern box
Box Manufacturer: St. Joe Paper Co. – Container Div., So. Hackensack, N.J.
Date Printed: None; 7
Months Printed: 6, 7, 8, 9, 10, 11, 12; 7, 8, 9, 10, 11, 12
Box Part Number: ?
Box Dimensions: 12½ x 18¼ x 7⅛

2291W **2379 Rio Grande, AB** **5 car freight** **81.25**
Box Type: Plain picture box
Box Manufacturer: Gibraltar Corrugated Paper Co., North Bergen, N.J.
Date Printed: Not Shown
Months Printed: Not Shown
Box Part Number: Not Shown
Box Dimensions: 14½ x 16 x 6¾

2296W **2373 Canadian Pacific, AA** **4 car pass.** **100.00**
Box Type: Plain picture box
Box Manufacturer: Gilbraltar Corrugated Paper Co., North Bergen, N.J.
Date Printed: Not Shown
Months Printed: Not Shown
Box Part Number: Not Shown
Box Dimensions: 11¼ x 20¾ x 7½

1958 F3 SETS

2507W **2242 New Haven, AB** **5 car freight** **65.00**
Box Type: Plain picture box
Box Manufacturer: Gibraltar Corrugated Paper Co., North Bergen, N.J.
Date Printed: Not Shown
Months Printed: Not Shown
Box Part Number: Not Shown
Box Dimensions: 12½ x 15¾ or 16 x 7

2517W **2379 Rio Grande, AB** **5 car freight** **75.00**
Box Type: Plain picture box
Box Manufacturer: Gibraltar Corrugated Paper Co., North Bergen, N.J.
Date Printed: Not Shown
Months Printed: Not Shown
Box Part Number: ?
Box Dimensions: 13½ x 15¾ x 6¾

2523W **2383 Santa Fe, AA** **5 car frtt/Acc** **95.00**
Box Type: Plain picture box
Box Manufacturer: Gibraltar Corrugated Paper Co., North Bergen, N.J.
Date Printed: Not Shown
Months Printed: Not Shown
Box Part Number: Not Shown
Box Dimensions: 16 x 17½ x 9½

2526W **2383 Santa Fe, AA** **4 car pass.** **100.00**
Box Type: Plain picture box
Box Manufacturer: Gibraltar Corrugated Paper Co., Inc., North Bergen, N.J.
Date Printed: Not Shown
Months Printed: Not Shown
Box Part Number: Not Shown
Box Dimensions: 12¾ x 17½ x 8¼

1959 F3 SETS

2537W **2242 New Haven, AB** **5 car freight** **75.00**
Box Type: Yellow generic box
Box Manufacturer: Star Corrugated Box Co., Inc., Maspeth, L.I., N.Y.
Date Printed: Not Shown
Months Printed: Not Shown
Box Part Number: Not Shown
Box Dimensions: 13 x 15½ x 7¼

2541W **2383 Santa Fe, AA** **5 car frt/Acc** **89.95**
Box Type: Yellow picture box
Box Manufacturer: Star Corrugated, Maspeth, L.I., N.Y.
Date Printed: Not Shown
Months Printed: Not Shown
Box Part Number: ?
Box Dimensions: 14¾ x 16¾ x 7¼

2544W **2383 Santa Fe, AA** **4 car pass.** **100.00**
Box Type: Yellow picture box
Box Manufacturer: Star Corrugated Box Co., Inc., Maspeth, L.I., N.Y.
Date Printed: Not Shown
Months Printed: Not Shown
Box Part Number: Not Shown
Box Dimensions: 12 x 20 x 7½

During 1955–1957, Lionel used both 3- and 4-digit numbers to designate identical sets, such as 819 and 2281W shown above.

1960 F3 SETS

2544W **2383 Santa Fe, AA** **4 car pass.** **100.00**
Box Type: Orange picture box
Box Manufacturer: Kraft Corrugated Containers, Inc., Bayonne, N.J.
Date Printed: Not Shown
Months Printed: Not Shown
Box Part Number: M5200 (Inner Flap)(one small flap)
Box Dimensions: 11½ x 20 x 7½

2555W **2383 Santa Fe, AA** **Over & Under** **150.00**
Box Type: Plain w/1 no. 2555W
Box Manufacturer: Star Corrugated Box Co., Inc., Maspeth, L.I., N.Y.
Date Printed: 9-60V
Months Printed: 9-60V
Box Part Number: 60-270
Box Dimensions: 15½ x 26 x 9⅝

1961 F3 SETS

2574 2383 Santa Fe, AA 5 car frr/Acc 89.95
Box Type: Orange picture box
Box Manufacturer: Mead Corporation, North Bergen, N.J.
Date Printed: Not Shown
Months Printed: Not Shown
Box Part Number: Not Shown
Box Dimensions: 15½ x 15¾ x 7

2576 2383 Santa Fe, AA 4 car pass. 100.00
Box Type: Plain, rubber-stamped no. 2576
Box Manufacturer: United Container Co., Philadelphia, Pa.
Date Printed: Not Shown
Months Printed: Not Shown
Box Part Number: ?
Box Dimensions: 13¼ x 17½ x 7½

1962 F3 SETS

13058 2383 Santa Fe, AA 5 car frt/Acc 89.95
Box Type: Orange generic box
Box Manufacturer: Mead Containers, North Bergen, N.J.
Date Printed: Not Shown
Months Printed: Not Shown
Box Part Number: ?
Box Dimensions: 16 x 17½ x 7

13088 2383 Santa Fe, AA 4 car pass. 120.00
Box Type: Brown/plain; end of box reads "1 No. 13088"
Box Manufacturer: Mead Containers, North Bergen, N.J.
Date Printed: None
Months Printed: None
Box Part Number: None
Box Dimensions: 13¼ x 17½ x 7½

1963 F3 SETS

13128 2383 Santa Fe, AA 5 car frt/Acc 89.95
Box Type: Orange generic, rubber-stamped 13128
Box Manufacturer: The Mead Corporation, North Bergen, N.J.
Date Printed: Not Shown
Months Printed: Not Shown
Box Part Number: 61-230
Box Dimensions: 15½ x 16 x 7¼

13148 2383 Santa Fe, AA 4 car pass. 120.00
Box Type: Plain generic, rubber-stamped 13148
Box Manufacturer: The Mead Corporation, North Bergen, N.J.
Date Printed: Not Shown
Months Printed: Not Shown
Box Part Number: Not Shown
Box Dimensions: 13⅛ x 17½ x 7

1964 F3 SETS

12720 2383 Santa Fe, AA 5 car freight 65.00
Box Type: Orange generic, rubber-stamped 12720
Box Manufacturer: The Mead Corp., North Bergen, N.J.
Date Printed: Not Shown
Months Printed: Not Shown
Box Part Number: 61-220 (on bottom flap)
Box Dimensions: 13 x 16 x 6

12730 2383 Santa Fe, AA 5 car freight 79.95
Box Type: Plain brown generic w/rubber-stamped 12730
Box Manufacturer: Robbins Container Corp., Brooklyn, N.Y.
Date Printed: Not Shown
Months Printed: Not Shown
Box Part Number: 18-8
Box Dimensions: 14½ x 18 x 8¼

12740 2383 Santa Fe, AA 7 car freight 79.95
Box Type:
Box Manufacturer:
Date Printed:
Months Printed:
Box Part Number:
Box Dimensions:

12750 2383 Santa Fe, AA 7 car freight 95.00
Box Type:
Box Manufacturer:
Date Printed:
Months Printed:
Box Part Number:
Box Dimensions:

12780 2383 Santa Fe, AA 4 car pass. 120.00
Box Type: Plain white generic, rubber-stamped 12780
Box Manufacturer: United Container Co., Philadelphia, Pa.
Date Printed: 3
Months Printed: Not Shown (Note: has The Lionel Corporation)
Box Part Number: 18-8
Box Dimensions: 13¼ x 17½ x 7

1965 F3 SETS

12730 2383 Santa Fe, AA 5 car freight 85.00
Box Type: Plain white generic w/rubber-stamped 12730
Box Manufacturer: United Container Corp., Philadelphia, Pa.
Date Printed: 65..........4..........
Months Printed: Not Shown (Note: has The Lionel Toy Corporation)
Box Part Number: None
Box Dimensions: 14¾ x 16 x 7

12780 2383 Santa Fe, AA 4 car pass. 125.00
Box Type: Plain white generic w/rubber-stamped 12780
Box Manufacturer: United Container Co., Philadelphia, Pa.
Date Printed: 65.....4.....
Months Printed: Not Shown
Box Part Number: None
Box Dimensions: 13½ x 17½ x 8

1966 F3 SETS

12730 2383 Santa Fe, AA 5 car freight 90.00
Box Type:
Box Manufacturer:
Date Printed:
Months Printed:
Box Part Number:
Box Dimensions:

12780 2383 Santa Fe, AA 4 car pass. 125.00
Box Type: Plain white generic
Box Manufacturer: United Container Co., Philadelphia, Pa.
Date Printed: 3 **** 66 ***
Months Printed: Not Shown
Box Part Number: 66 108
Box Dimensions: 14¼ x 26 x 8¼

12780 2383 Santa Fe, AA 4 car pass. 125.00
Box Type: Plain brown w/rubber-stamped 12780
Box Manufacturer: Robbins Container Corp., Brooklyn, N.Y.
Date Printed: Not Shown
Months Printed: Not Shown
Box Part Number: 18-8
Box Dimensions: 14½ x 18 x 8¼

Box Nomenclature for Postwar Paper-type Boxes

Early Classic: The most notable box of the Postwar era introduced in 1948 for the 027 line with smaller lettering; the city names "New York," "Chicago," and "San Francisco"; and with the stock name printed on all four sides.

Middle Classic: Same as Early Classic, except the city name of "San Francisco" was eliminated. It was used from mid-1949 though 1955.

OPS Classic: Same as Middle Classic, but with the inclusion of the OPS stamp. It was used in 1952.

Late Classic: Same as Middle Classic, except that the stock number was omitted from the four sides. It was used from 1956 through 1958.

Bold Classic: Same as Late Classic, but with a much bolder-faced print on the end flaps. It was used for part of the 1958 product line.

Excerpted from *Greenberg's Guide to Lionel Trains, 1945–1969: Volume III, Sets*, by Paul V. Ambrose, Greenberg Publishing Co., 1990.

The word "generic" is used to describe Lionel boxes designed for multiple purposes – "one size fits all." They were in common use for F3 set boxes by the early to mid 1960s.